SELLERS

OF

DREAMS

Fifty years of advertising beauty products

Ruth Artmonsky

Published by:
Artmonsky Arts
Flat 1, 27 Henrietta Street
London WC2E 8NA
artmonskyruth@gmail.com
Tel. 020 7240 8774

Text © Ruth Artmonsky 2020

ISBN 978-1-9163845-2-1

Designed by:
David Preston Studio
www.davidprestonstudio.com

Printed in England by:
Northend Creative Print Solutions
www.northend.co.uk

As usual, my thanks go to my designers David and Tamsin at David Preston Studio for their innovation and wit.

Contents

RADIANCE brings her loveliness to life. Her skin has a glow beneath its creamy finish, her lips are a smooth brilliance.

Where she moves the sun seems to shine. This beauty is of her own making, her own intelligent choosing.

Elizabeth Hellier

Airspun Face Powder made by a new, modern process, exclusive to Coty, 3/-. Coty Sub-tint (powder base) gives a vibrant underglow, in five shades, 6/8 and 2/6. Coty Cream Rouge and Powder Rouge, 3/11. Coty Creamy Lipstick, firm, smooth and brilliant, 7/5. Quick-change refill, 3/11.

Coty

FOR BEAUTY

AT ALL GOOD SHOPS AND AT THE COTY SALON, 3 NEW BOND STREET, W.1

Left: 'Coty for beauty' advert, *Harper's Bazaar*, 1951.

Introduction

Faced with self-isolation in February 2020, at the start of the pandemic, being well into the aged 'at risk' group, I knew I needed a challenge to occupy myself for what could be months ahead. I had just finished a book, was working on another with my designer, but one that had a notional deadline, so I could foresee a blank diary ahead.

I had previously thought of extending my interest in the design of mid-twentieth century advertising to that for beauty products, but with a handbag full of pills, hearing aid accessories, and other props to old age, with not a cream or lipstick in sight, I hesitated to venture into such relatively unknown, or unknown to me, territory.

I then thought of the horror beyond my walls and the serious sacrifices that were being made and began to consider that the small amount of mental pain I might endure researching a subject that had little interest for me personally, when my whole point of writing at all was to have fun, was worth the alternative of weeks of television and boredom.

Against expectations I have found the beauty product industry, its chancers and exploiters, well worth getting out of bed early each day for. What I had hesitated to start on became a welcome lockdown occupation, became a near obsession with 'the sellers of dreams'.

The Way to Beauty

Skin

Pomeroy 'Guard your beauty' advert, *The Home Magazine*, 1925.

The marketing ploys of manufacturers of skin products can be encapsulated in the history of one firm. One, Theron T. Pond, an American pharmacist, along with his investors, established the firm T.T. Pond & Co. in 1849 on the strength of two creams Theron had developed – Pond's Cold Cream and Pond's Vanishing Cream – one for the day, the other for the night. By the 1880s these creams were being advertised fiercely with the tag 'Every normal skin needs these two creams'. At its zenith Pond's was advertising in well over one hundred countries, with 10 creams, five facial foams, six talcum powders, 14 facial cleaners, eight facial moisturisers and eight make-up removers on offer; not to even start on its powders. Once manufacturers realized the gold mine, everyone was on the bandwagon.

Women were assured that to beautify the skin they needed creams to open the pores, cleanse pores, close pores, tighten it, moisturise it, cover its blemishes, protect it from weather, and, in addition, give it the necessary powders and rouges that the fashion of the time demanded. When to these considerations are added whether

Above: Signage designed by Macdonald Gill for Pomeroy, c. 1924.

Opposite page, left: Poster designed by Edward McKnight Kauffer for Pomeroy, c. 1926.

Opposite page, right: Advert for 'Dubarry's Complexion Creams', *The Strand Magazine*, December 1931.

the product should be used by night (not to be seen) or by day (could be visible), and that different qualities of products would be needed for different textures of skin and colour, the combinations and permutations could be endless; what a bonanza.

As Britain was to trail France when it came to perfumes, it was to trail America when it came to skin care. Nevertheless, even before WWI two British firms were pioneering products for the skin – creams, powders and rouges. These were both run by women, Mrs. Hemming, who established Cyclax in South Moulton Street in 1897, and Jeanette Scale (who changed her name to Pomeroy) who set up the beauty business bearing that name in Old Bond Street in 1895 (it must be admitted that Mrs. Pomeroy was actually American, only British by marriage).

Mrs. Pomeroy tended to stress the remedial nature of her goods, their hygienic production and their purifying qualities, especially for tackling wrinkles and blemishes. Soon Pomeroy Complexion Purifier, Pomeroy Skin Food, Pomeroy Oatmeal, Pomeroy Face Powder, Pomeroy Liquid Powder and Pomeroy Liquid Rouge were on the market, available by mail order. Pomeroy Rouge was offered in a range of colours – almond blossom, Pomeroy Pink, Coral, Russet, Fantasy, Red Cap, Tudor Rose and Cherry. Although Mrs. Pomeroy was to sell out, Pomeroy skin care products were still being advertised from Bond Street through until after WWII. Much of the pre-war

JEANNETTE POMEROY BEAUTY PRODUCTS
174 NEW BOND STREET, W.1

SKIN FOOD · BEAUTY MILK · CLEANSING CREAM · DAY CREAM
DATHOS · POWDER · LIPSTICK · SAFADA HAND LOTION *Prices from 3/6 to 16/6*

Ten minutes a day
to hold elusive beauty.

ARE you one of many women who has longed for a clear, beautiful skin?—a skin that will be the envy of others?—a skin that will be admired wherever you go?

Glorious beauty is within easy reach. By spending ten minutes a day using Cyclax Beauty Preparations, yours will be a healthy, glowing skin that speaks of youthful loveliness. The method is simple, because it is based on the laws of nature. It is the treatment originated by Mrs. Hemming, the world-famous beauty consultant, of the Cyclax Beauty Salons, who for years has advised and treated Royalty, those whose names appear on the social register, and famous actresses.

For a thorough understanding of the results and the method, call at the Cyclax Salons for a trial sitting. The price is only 12/6. At the end of the treatment look at yourself in the mirror and see how much clearer your skin has become. Notice how fresh and renewed it feels. Nothing but natural methods are used—no artificial aids—only simple, normal processes that take away impurities, soothe tissues, and brace muscles.

Distance need not prevent you from taking advantage of Mrs. Hemming's advice and the help of her expert assistants. Write her a letter and state your skin troubles—describing the faults and general character—and she will explain how to correct its condition, and tell you where to secure the necessary Cyclax Beauty Preparations. Ask, too, for a complimentary copy of her own helpful book, "The Cultivation and Preservation of Natural Beauty."

Home Treatment "Cyclax" Preparations

"CYCLAX" SKIN FOOD is the only cream which is bracing and nourishing. Price 4/- and 7/6

"CYCLAX" BLENDED LOTION imparts a beautiful surface to the skin and is most nourishing & protective. Price 4/6 & 8/6

"CYCLAX" SPECIAL LOTION clears the skin from all impurity and produces a flawless complexion. Price 8/6 and 10/6

"CYCLAX" FACE POWDER is the finest face powder created, and is most beautiful to the skin. Price 6/6

Mrs. Hemming's

'Cyclax' Beauty Preparations
"CYCLAX" (Mrs. Hemming)

13 & 14 (D), New Bond Street, London, W.1 (Regent 2563)
58 (D), South Molton Street, London, W.1 (Mayfair 3972)

PARIS, NEW YORK,
CALCUTTA, EDINBURGH,
LIVERPOOL, ETC.

A. & P.S.—80.

Above: Cyclax, *Eve*, July 1924.

Opposite page: 'Pomeroy serves beauty' advert, *Housewife* magazine, February 1945.

advertising was handled by the Westminster Press, with posters created by such outstanding graphic designers as Edward McKnight Kauffer, many bearing the tag 'helps the plain, improves the fair'!

Mrs. Hemming had her range on the market by 1902, and, was said to be producing some forty items, including creams and powders, selling across Europe; indeed across the Empire. Eventually Cyclax bought up Pomeroy but was, in turn, purchased by Lehman Bros. and then sold on. As with Pomeroy, Cyclax appears to have had a generous advertising budget, and also sold through beauty salons. Cyclax seems to have relied rather more on its copywriters than its graphic designers for it's advertising, as with the following example:

Glorious beauty is within every reach. By spending ten minutes a day using Cyclax beauty preparations, you will be youthful loveliness. The method is simple because it is based on the laws of nature. It is the treatment originated by Mrs. Hemming the world famous beauty consultant, of the Cyclax beauty salons, who for years has advised and treated Royalty, those whose names appear in the social register, and famous actresses.

British skin care products that needed no special pleading that medically approved ingredients were being used were those in the Boots No.7 range, launched in 1935 as 'the modern way to loveliness'. No.7 was definitely for the mass market, with a Boots chemist shop of nearly every high street. As with Pond's, Boots started with a

So much lovelier...
your skin with
GlamOtint

Because GlamOtint touches your face to beauty lightly, delicately...

Because this creamy liquid foundation smooths on easily, evenly, adding enchanting warmth and colour...

Because it never cakes, never streaks, always looks and feels natural as your skin...

And because it needs only occasional touch-ups with matching Cyclax Beauty Pressed powder to keep your complexion morning-fresh and shine-free until bedtime...

Your skin will never look lovelier than it will with GlamOtint, the perfect foundation for every type of skin.

Six complexion tints:
Pink Velvet, Rose Velvet, Peach Velvet, Bronze Velvet, Cream Velvet and Tan Velvet.   8/6 and 13/10.

Cyclax OF LONDON
the finest beauty preparations and cosmetics in the world.

LONDON SALON: 58 SOUTH MOLTON STREET, W.1

Would he marry me again?

My husband used to call my complexion 'peaches-and-cream'. But after our baby was born he'd have said skim-milk-and-lemon, if he said anything at all. I was pretty discouraged until I discovered the little miracle that a quick freshener with Number Seven Complexion Milk brought about. Then a bright dash of Number Seven Cherry Ripe Lipstick, and compliments came my way again.

Housewife or career girl—there's an answer to your complexion problems in the honey and gold containers of the new Number Seven preparations. Ask the cosmetic assistant at Boots to show you the creams and lotions for your skin type—the individual make up that's perfect for *you*.

NEW...better and lovelier
NUMBER SEVEN
BEAUTY PREPARATIONS

CLEANSING CREAM, 5/- · COMPLEXION MILK, 4/-
EXTRA-RICH SKIN FOOD, 5/- · SKIN FRESHENER, 6/-
MAKE-UP BASE, 4/- · CREAM FOUNDATION, 5/-
TONE-UP LOTION, 6/- · VANISHING CREAM, 5/-
FACE POWDER, 5/- · LIPSTICK, 6/6 · REFILL, 2/6

Made and sold by Boots

Far left: Cyclax advertisement for GlamOtint liquid foundation, *Vanity Fair*, October 1956.

Left: 'Would he marry me again?' advertisement for Number Seven, Boots own cosmetics range, *Vogue* magazine, December 1952.

presents
LIQUID BEAUTY

Dawn - to - dusk loveliness! This new glamorous liquid foundation brings to *every* skin natural loveliness. And Goya face powder, blending softly with this non-drying liquid, flatters the skin for hours without retouching. Liquid Beauty, in Natural (untinted) Light, Medium, Brunette. 5/-. Goya Face Powder in six lovely shades. 2/9.

G O Y A   P A R I S   L O N D O N   N E W   Y O R K

Above: 'Goya presents liquid beauty' by René Gruau, *Woman's Journal*, October 1953.

small range of items but a post-war advertisement for No.7 listed, besides lipsticks, eye-make-up and the like, some nine offerings just for the skin – cleansing cream, complexion milk, extra-rich skin food, skin freshener, make-up base, cream foundation, tone-up lotion, vanishing cream and face powder.

Yet another British company, Goya, founded in the 1930s, also established itself in Bond Street. Although starting out as a perfumer, by the 1940s it had a fully developed range of preparations for the skin. Although perfume continued to be its mainstay by the post-war years it had on the market powder (some six lovely shades) and four liquid creams:

> They just melt into the skin. Liquid cleanser melts in and floats out dirt. Liquid skin food melts in and nourishes deep. Liquid foundation forms the smoothest powder base ever known.

Goya had the budget to use René Gruau, the iconic French designer, for it's advertising, pitching its ware at the sophisticated end of the market – the evening-gown end. A number of the companies used

After the Wear and Tear

In the twentieth century "the day's wear and tear" is a very real thing, and the woman who desires to keep young in appearance must perform a little ceremony every night if the beauty of her complexion is not to be sacrificed. She must massage a little of Pond's Cold Cream into the skin of her face, neck, arms and hands.

What effect has this nightly massage?

It cleanses the pores of the skin far more efficiently than soap and water alone can do. It makes the skin soft yet firm, free from roughness and lines—gives it every night an added touch of youthfulness retained or even returned.

Present-day conditions render the use of a day cream strongly advisable. Pond's Vanishing Cream is without a serious rival as a refresher of tired, jaded complexions, a protector against wind, rain, and dust, and is an essential base for powder.

"*TO SMOOTH AND SOOTHE YOUR SKIN.*"

Both creams obtainable from all chemists and stores in oval jars at **1/3** *and* **2/6**, *and in collapsible tubes, price* **7½d.** *(hand-bag size) and* **1/-.**

FREE SAMPLES.	Pond's Extract Company will send on receipt of 3d. in stamps for postage and packing, a sample tube of Vanishing Cream and Cold Cream containing a liberal supply.

POND'S EXTRACT CO., 71, Southampton Row, London, W.C.1.

Pond's Cold Cream

the analogy of food and nourishment in their advertising of beauty products, but the American Food and Drugs Act soon banned that as fallacious.

The American skin products market was dominated by a number of feisty women: at the upper end Helena Rubinstein, Elizabeth Arden, Dorothy Gray, and in the post-war years Estée Lauder. More popularly pitched were the men manufacturers, Max Factor and Charles Revson of Revlon. Pond's was definitely aiming at the mass market.

Pond's had been founded in 1849, Mr. Pond, himself, dying in 1852. Continuing with the brand name, it used much press advertising and, from the 1910s was relying on J. Walter Thompson. Peter and Polly Ponds were devised as representing the man and woman in the street, as the potential buyers of its magical two skin creams. After WWI Pond's seems to have wanted to shift itself more up-market and, for the British market, its advertising which had appeared in such modest journals as *Home Notes* and *Home Magazine* began to carry images of Lady this and Lady that and even the odd Countess. Lady Patricia French, 'the glamorous grand-daughter of the famous Commander-in-Chief of the British Forces in France in 1914' declares:

I use Pond's Cold Cream every night for that's the best way to get dirt and make-up from my skin so that skin blemishes don't come. I use Pond's Vanishing Cream before powdering. It smooths away any roughness at once and holds powder a

17

You need
the protection
of POND'S

During your holiday more than at any other time you need *Pond's Vanishing Cream*. It protects from sunburn and the harshening effects of sea water, gives the skin a beautiful bloom, and makes a lasting and reliable base for your powder. Used in conjunction with *Pond's Cold Cream*, *Pond's Cleansing Tissues*, and *Pond's Skin Freshener*, it keeps the skin fine and smooth and the complexion beautifully clear. If you are not already a user of these preparations, send 1/- to Pond's Extract Co., (Dept. 504,) 103, St. John St., London, E.C.1, who will send you a four-sample package to try.

OBTAINABLE FROM CHEMISTS, STORES & HIGH CLASS HAIRDRESSERS.

Pond's Vanishing Cream, Opal Jars, 2/6 and 1/3. Tubes 1/- and 6d.
Pond's Cold Cream, Opal Jars, 5/-, 2/6 and 1/3. Tubes, 2/6, 1/- and 6d.
Pond's Cleansing Tissues, per box, 2/-, 1/3, & 9d.
Pond's Skin Freshener, per bottle, 5/6, 3/- & 1/-

Pond's

COLD CREAM,
CLEANSING TISSUES,
SKIN FRESHENER,
VANISHING CREAM.

Left: 'You need the protection of Pond's', *Home Chat*, August 1929.

Below: Pond's advertisement, *Woman's Journal*, May 1935.

in spite of cutting sea winds
... her skin is petal-smooth

THE LADY STANLEY OF ALDERLEY

If you could see Lady Stanley of Alderley in the evening, her red-gold hair gleaming in the lights, her shoulders white against a topaz gown, how you'd exclaim at the beauty of her skin ! You'd think that rough winds, dust and burning sun never had a chance to reach her face. You'd say " She must spend pounds on beauty treatments to keep her skin so fresh and lovely."

But Lady Stanley is wiser than that. " I'm much too busy to spend hours in beauty parlours," she says, " I sail a lot. And I've found that with Pond's Creams I can keep my skin in perfect condition — on the yacht or ashore.

" As a protection against biting winds and spray, Pond's Creams are better than the most elaborate beauty treatments. Every night I spread the Cold Cream over my face and neck, and leave it on a few minutes. It softens the dirt and impurities that clog up the pores, and floats them gently to the surface — ready to be wiped away.

" Always before powdering I smooth Pond's Vanishing Cream over my face and neck. I need never worry then about getting rough and chapped and lined, after a day's sailing." This foamy Cream restores natural freshness to the skin which winds and heated rooms tend to dry out.

Use Pond's Creams for yourself ! They'll make your complexion as lovely as this Society Leader's. Though the choice of so many wealthy women, these creams are very inexpensive. Trial jars and tubes are only 6d.

POND'S

The one cream every woman should use!

Beauty Overnight Cream

does more for your skin in two weeks than two years normal care

Beauty Overnight Cream feeds your skin precious moisture and vital nourishing ingredients while you sleep. Awakens your complexion to lasting loveliness through safe, natural skin feeding. For all types of skin . . . all ages of beauty. 12/-.

MOISTURISE DAY & NIGHT WITH SKIN DEW
New French Formula acts in 10 seconds to deep-moisturise away all signs of dryness. Use beneath your daytime foundation *and* before bed. Popular new 12/6 size, and 23/-.

Helena Rubinstein

J GRAFTON STREET, LONDON, W.1 PARIS NEW YORK

Above: 'Beauty Overnight Cream', advertisement for Helena Rubinstein, *Home*, May 1961.

long time. Now that these creams contain the 'skin vitamin' they seem almost miraculous! They've made my complexion exceptionally clear and smooth, made pores smaller and softened away little lines.

For these 'titled women' advertising campaigns Ponds was to continue to use J. Walter Thompson and its senior famed creative director Helen Lansdowne Resor.

Helena Rubinstein and Elizabeth Arden, unlike Pond's, were determined to be classy from the start, the former oftimes presenting a slightly medical slant when advertising, with much mention of 'formulae' and herself portrayed in a white laboratory coat. Elizabeth Arden went for a more 'outdoor' girl image, fresh and free, although she had all her beauty clinic staff dressed in 'medical' white coats and shoes, not missing that trick. Lindy Woodhead described both women as: 'tyrannical, temperamental, obsessive, mercurial, despotic workaholics'. And this certainly is communicated in their advertising. It is said that account executives from advertising agencies would take phenobarbital before meetings with Arden, to steel themselves.

Of the two, Arden was the more committed to advertising and to advertising and developing her business in Britain. Whereas Rubinstein would work through her press office and through agencies as, latterly, David Ogilvy, Arden was very much in control, down to the last detail. She made use of agencies, as the Blake Agency in New York, and Colman, Prentis, & Varley (CPV) in

Below: 'For the girl who's
going places', advert for Helena
Rubinstein, *Home*, May 1961.

For the girl who's going places . . .

be pretty
in a
minute!

Silk
Minute Make-up

First all-in-one moisturising make-up

IT isn't nice to keep love waiting! So the girl who's always
going places is ready in 60-seconds with Silk Minute
Make-Up. It glides on . . . covers tiny imperfections with a
radiant veil of pure atomised silk blended with a special silken
foundation. Like silk it flatters . . . like silk it glows . . . like
silk it clings to your skin. And only Silk Minute Make-Up
contains special moisture-retaining ingredients to keep your
complexion marvellously soft and supple . . . to beauty-treat
your skin all day long.

*Silk Minute Make-Up in the square-cut compact 10/-, refills 6/3
also Silk Minute Make-Up Special for Dry Skins 10/-, refills 6/3.*

NEW *Heart-Shape Lipstick fits your lips like a Kiss !* Out-
lines, fills in, in one fluent gesture. Exciting new colours,
especially Heart of Pink for blondes . . . reckless Heart of
Red for brunettes! Scratchproof Satin Gilt case 10/6. Refills
(Plastic case) 6/6.

Helena Rubinstein

J GRAFTON STREET, LONDON, W.1 · PARIS · NEW YORK

London, but would check everything herself and vetoed constantly what did not meet her requirements. In the early years she had actually done much of the copywriting herself, but came to rely on Henry Sell, an ex-editor of *Harper's Bazaar*, who had bought the Blake agency. She was to use Sell through to WWII but fired him in the post-war years. Sell would refer to her snidely as 'our lady of lotions'. At the peak of Elizabeth Arden's business she is said to have had some seventy-five items in her range, including creams for every purpose possible, along with her 'eight hour cream' that was claimed to do it all.

Both Arden and Rubinstein were looking to an elite market, advertising in the classiest magazines, and using the best emerging artists and photographers for their publicity; both set up establishments in Mayfair. Arden's success in Britain ('brought by royalty') was partly aided by her obsession with horses, buying and training some of her horses in England and Ireland, which inevitably brought her in touch with useful contacts. But she was well supported by her London manager, Teddy Haslam (taken from Harrods), an establishment personality who, like Sells, was to remain loyal to Arden for decades.

When CPV let Lord Montagu of Beaulieu loose on Arden in New York, she was captivated, and wrote that '(he) has been urging me to create special coronation year preparations…'. And, indeed, the 'English Complexion' range duly appeared, a powder foundation, rouge and two powders, which were to be used alongside her best

Below: Advertisement for
Elizabeth Arden, *c.* 1922.

Right: Elizabeth Arden, *Illustrated
London News*, May 1937.

English Complexion

This is an English year in Paris and New York as well as in London. The English
beauty is the beauty of the season. Her favourite colours, chosen to accentuate
her clear complexion, are the mode. To help you achieve her delicate, fragile
loveliness, Miss Arden has devised the new "English Complexion" make-up.
*Make-up requirements:—*Powder foundation—Naturelle Lille Lotion; Rouge, Lipstick,
Nail Varnish—Coquette; 1st Powder—Ardena Mat Foncé; 2nd Powder—Japonica
'Lysetta'; Eyeshado—Gris Brun and Bleu Vert, with Black Cosmetique to complete
the effect. But beneath the make-up you must have a flawless skin. Keep it
fresh and young by faithfully using these essential preparations for CLEANSING:
Venetian Cleansing Cream; 4/6 to 22/6 TONING: *Ardena Skin Tonic; 3/6 to 75/-*
SOOTHING: *Ardena Velva Cream; 4/6 to 22/6* *Orange Skin Food; 4/6 to 35/-*

2 5   O L D   B O N D   S T R E E T   L O N D O N   W E S T   O N E

21

Above: Publicity for Elizabeth Arden, with artwork by Francis Marshall, 1938.

Opposite page, left: Advertisement for Elizabeth Arden, with artwork by René Gruau, 1953.

Opposite page, right: 'Just doing is a joy', Elizabeth Arden, *Vogue*, February 1967.

sellers – Venetian Cleansing Cream, Ardena Skin Tonic, Ardena Velva Cream and Orange Skin Food. In its advertising of the time it made much use of the royal event.

Neither Arden nor Rubinstein descended to marketing using blatant sex. Arden's women, as portrayed in her advertising, were 'superior' – well-dressed, even haughty in pose – sometimes drawn by Gruau; rarely does a man appear, even in the background. Rubinstein began to include men in the 1950s and '60s for its 'Silk' make-up campaigns, but even then, there was rarely even a hint that applying creams and powders was going to help one find 'Mr. Right'.

Nor did Estée Lauder resort to using the ploy of sexual attraction when she launched Estée Lauder Cosmetics in 1946. Geoffrey Jones describes her as imaging 'elegant achievers' rather than 'sex kittens'. Although, in America, she resorted to slightly down market mail shots and 'gifts with purchases' her first international account was with Harrods and her advertisements were placed in *Vogue*.

Max Factor, a Polish émigré to the States, a wigmaker who settled in Hollywood having arrived via the Imperial Russian Grand Opera, was rather more prepared to cash in on 'romance' if not 'blatant' sexual attraction in his advertising. Initially specializing in make-up for the motion picture industry from about 1914, by the 1920s he had widened his target to the mass market. A 1937 advertisement in *Woman's Journal* for face powder and rouge carried a photograph of Gary Cooper and Madeleine Caroll with the tag 'her

Elizabeth Arden

ARDENA CLEANSING
CREAM for pore-deep
cleanliness, immaculate
freshness. 8/3, 14/9, 22/6

ARDENA SKIN TONIC
delightfully bracing,
mildly astringent, helps
to clear and brighten
the skin. 8/3, 17/6, 33/9

ORANGE SKIN FOOD.
A rich emollient cream,
for the normal or dry
skin. 8/3, 14/9, 22/6

ARDENA SPECIAL
HORMONE CREAM
revitalises, keeps the
skin fresh, younger
looking. 25/-, 42/6

Coronation Year can be a memorable one for the wise woman
who looks to Miss Arden's Beauty Ritual—CLEANSE, TONE, NOURISH
—to make her complexion radiantly lovely. Used regularly as she
advises, Miss Arden's famous "essentials" give to the skin clarity, smooth
texture and that cherished, cared-for look.
And for those who remember other Coronation years—the "over-thirties"—
there is ARDENA SPECIAL HORMONE CREAM, designed to give back to the skin the
vital substances of which nature's own supply begins to slow down after thirty.

Visit our Elizabeth Arden Salon for REFRESHING FACE TREATMENTS

*The
Elizabeth Arden
way to beauty—
just doing it is a joy*

The Elizabeth Arden way to beauty is not just a beauty routine, it's a delicious
ceremony in itself. Surrounding yourself with little jars and bottles, their
delicate fragrance tinting the room, it takes you just a few minutes. First,
the pleasure of liquefying Ardena Cleansing Cream...then the zip of Ardena
Skin Tonic and finally, a silky application of Orange Skin Food or Crème
Extrordinaire to nourish and smooth away those unwanted wrinkles. Cleanse,
tone, nourish—every day—to bring a new bloom and loveliness to your skin.

Elizabeth Arden
25 Old Bond St., London, W.1.

23

So much smoother . . . so much less greasy than ordinary 'vanishing' creams . . .

Max Factor's Invisible Make-Up Foundation

Holds your powder . . . for hours and hours

Protects your complexion . . . keeps it soft and smooth

Stays matt . . . with never a trace of shine

Max Factor brings to you in this wonderfully smooth Invisible Make-Up Foundation yet another of the beauty secrets of Hollywood's loveliest Stars. Just spread oh-so-little over your face and neck . . . and your skin is given day-long protection against the harmful ageing effects of wind, dust and sun . . . your complexion remains smooth, clear and matt with never a trace of shine . . . your powder is held firmly without need for repair or replacement. Try Max Factor Invisible Make-Up Foundation today! . . . the very foundation of your . . .

natural loveliness!

6/8

Max Factor
HOLLYWOOD

Opposite page: Various Max Factor adverts, from left to right, *Woman's Journal*, May 1937; *Housewife*, January 1944; and *Ideal Home*, July 1946.

Above: Advertisement for Max Factor's Invisible Make-Up Foundation, featuring actress Esther Williams, *Woman's Journal*, October 1953.

enchanting beauty fascinates men', and, for the reader of the advertisement:

In your life, as in the drama of life you see on the motion picture screen, beauty will help you win romance... and now you, like the screen stars, may share a new make-up secret which will enable you to make yourself more attractive, more lovely, almost instantly.

Max Factor had opened in Bond Street in 1935, but its greater impact in the British make-up industry came after WWII when Pan-Sticks were launched. Max Factor's Pancake (panchromatic) make-up was being developed in the 1930s, with lighter shades for general use by 1938, the year he died. The stick had the advantage that it was packaged, to be easily carried in a handbag, and easily applied by a swivel mechanism; it became a godsend for spotty adolescents.

Generally beauty products for the skin, in their advertising, focused nearly as much on anti-ageing as beautifying, although it could be easily argued the two aspects were related. Whilst Pond's carried such tags as 'big pores become invisible, blemishes go', it was also mentioning 'lines soften away'; Adelaide Grey's Laleek Rose Skin Food was more direct claiming its product 'nourishes and restores youth'; and, what must have been rather worrying for the majority of

25

Right: Nivea 'Creme or Oil'
advertisement, *Home Notes*,
August 1939.

Far right: 'You can always
tell a Nivea family!', *John Bull*,
May 1954.

readers, Gala recommending its hormone cream as bringing 'moist
young freshness to the over-thirty skin'!

With the 1920s came sunbathing, recommended by doctors
for one's health, and encouraged by the 'in' set as fashionable,
demonstrating that one could afford to luxuriate in hot climes,
particularly along the French Riviera. Previously, when a pale
complexion had been in vogue, women would appear at the seaside
with sunbonnets, veils and parasols. In the inter-war years when beach
clothing became scanty, sunbathing would frequently be accompanied
by sunburn. L'Oréal's Ambre Solaire, said to have been produced to

'Nivea for a carefree continental tan', *Vogue*, June 1969.

Advert for Sun-bronze by Charles of the Ritz, *The Queen*, June 1953.

Take every chance to bask in the summer sunshine but use Elizabeth Arden's special preparations to keep your skin cool, smooth and lovely while you tan.

ARDENA SUNPRUF CREAM...*filters out the burning rays of the sun to let you tan without discomfort* .. 5/9

EIGHT HOUR CREAM...*to smooth and cool your skin after unwise exposure* . . . 9/3

ARDENA POWDER... *in shades for Summer skins. Rose Rachel, Rosetta Bronze, Light Summer Sun,* 12/6, 20/9

Elizabeth Arden

NEW YORK 25 OLD BOND STREET, LONDON, W.1. PARIS

Elizabeth Arden, 'A place in the sun', *House & Garden*, July 1946.

YARDLEY ORCHIS POWDER

State Ball

Poise that would carry you triumphantly through the splendour and traditional elegance of State ceremonial can only spring from well-founded confidence in your appearance. Trust your complexion to the Yardley Orchis Powder.

Because it is so fine and clinging, and of such supreme quality, it will keep your complexion at its loveliest for hours

And, especially in English Peach shade, what soft warmth, and how flawless a finish it will give your skin ! You will delight, too, in the richness of its Orchis perfume ....

2/- LARGE BOX

ASK FOR THE SILVER BOX

YARDLEY · 33 OLD BOND STREET · LONDON

What is 'Captive Beauty'?

The wonderful new liquid vitaliser that braces and firms the contours of your face and smooths out that dry, lined look. You can feel its action at once. It makes the skin glow with vitality. Smooth in a few drops at night, and beneath your powder foundation by day. Captive Beauty makes you look radiant for parties and keeps your skin soft, supple and smooth in every kind of weather. Use it regularly, and even the most unemotional male will exclaim: 'You do look well!'

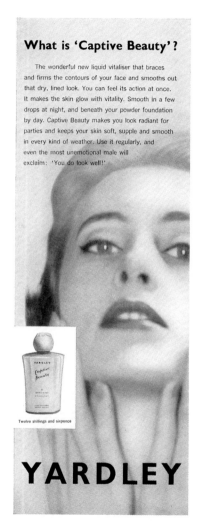

Twelve shillings and sixpence

YARDLEY

A
Slender
Stroke
of Genius

...the new slim-line
compact brimfull of
**YARDLEY
CREAM POWDER**
loveliness 5/4 ...
complete with puff
and mirror too!

YARDLEY

protect its Director, an avid sailor, from sunburn, from its start, was hyped as an antiseptic for sunburn, and, with its advertising in the hands of J. Walter Thompson, it was to become a significant player at the top end of the market.

Nivea, the cream for the masses, had originally been advertised, before WWII, as a general skin cream, and had adopted its familiar blue and white packaging by the mid-1920s. Advertising linking its application directly to sun protection seems to have come rather later, when to its long-term tag 'skin needs Nivea' was added 'a golden glow' and 'a carefree continental tan'. Other post-WWII competitors were Charles of the Ritz, definitely at the upper end of the market, placing its advertisements in journals as *The Queen* and such; and Cooltan with its advertisements appearing more frequently in the popular *Picture Post*, with its then winner, Kathie the Cooltan girl.

Opposite page, center: Yardley Orchis Powder, *Illustrated London News*, May 1935.

Opposite page, right: Yardley Captive Beauty, *The Queen*, February 1955.

Left: Yardley Cream Powder, *Vogue*, January 1967.

heiress
to beauty...

from mother to daughter,
generation to generation,
Steiner has become
a living legend of elegance,
offering service and fashion
as contemporary as the hour.

Hair

Although men and women earning their living by 'dressing' hair was common from the late eighteenth century, most women attended to their own hair as well as they could, or, if sufficiently well-off had their maids at hand. Salons, styling hair and selling hair grooming products, originally considered somewhat disreputable, did not really become popular until the twentieth century, particularly with the arrival of electrical means of perming and drying hair.

From the makers of soaps, from perfumers, from small time chemists, grew the international companies offering products that would beautify the hair – wash, treat, dye, condition, style, dry. Schwarzkopf, L'Oréal, Steiner, Proctor & Gamble, Unilever – all were to play a part in what was to become a major industry. In the early days their outlets were the hair salons, but as with other beautifying offerings, through strong advertising campaigns, hair products were brought to the masses, and sold through department stores, chains, chemist shops and, eventually, the corner store and supermarket.

The Leading Ladies' Hairdresser
(30 Private Salons)

Speciality
"ULTIMA"
THE FASCINATING
TRANSFORMATION

OTHER DEPTS FOR
Attendance
Permanent –
Waving
Tinting
Treatment
Ornaments
Manicure
Beauty Culture

WRITE FOR
ILLUSTRATED BROCHURE

ULTIMA

EMILE
of
Conduit St.

EMILE LTD, LONDON & PARIS.

Opposite page: Advert for Maison Nicol, *Eve*, July 1924.

Above: Emile of Conduit Street, *The Sketch*, March 1927.

Oftimes it was the professional hairdressers, the stylists, whose name became a brand in itself, beyond the brand name of particular products. Legros de Rumigny had been appointed court hairdresser in the mid-eighteenth century and, fast forward some two hundred years, French was still going to be the key to hairstylist branding. From the early 1920s with Emile of Conduit Street and Maison Nicol of New Bond Street through to the 1950s with Riché, Antoine, René and French of London (familiarly known as Freddie having served in the RAF); having a French name seems to have been a key to success to a hairdresser becoming a celebrity. How many of these gentlemen were actually French is questionable. French names abounded round Mayfair (as with plain Nigel Davies morphing into Justin de Villeneuve); Andres two a penny. It took Vidal Sassoon to break ranks, but even then his first name had a sufficiently exotic foreignness to attract.

Whether a stylist's name was French or not, dropping the odd French word into an advertisement gave a salon a piquancy. The word 'postiche' would occur where hairpieces were a speciality, as with Maison George of Buckingham Palace Road, who called his 'transformations' 'La Naturelle'. Most commonly used, of course, was the word 'coiffeur' – Emile describing himself as 'coiffeur artist', Riché a 'chef d'oeuvre de coiffeur', Alan Spires offering 'arts

"La Naturelle"
THE PERFECTLY NATURAL TRANSFORMATION

The unique world-famous "La Naturelle" transformation with its wonderful natural parting is absolutely undetectable in wear. Portfolio of new styles, with details of the "Times" system of payment by instalments, sent post free. Full transformation from 12 gns. Semi from 8 gns. Bobbed or long-haired head-dress from 18 gns.

Have your hair permanently waved by London's leading artistes who will take pleasure in arranging a style specially for you. There is distinction about a Maison Georges Coiffure. You will be delighted with its lasting beauty. Whole head 4 gns. Half-head 2½ gns. Side pieces, 1 gn. No charge is made for consultation and advice.

'Phone : Victoria 5943 and 5944

Telegrams : 'Toupetchic, Sowest, London'

Maison Georges
40. BUCKINGHAM PALACE R.D. LONDON S.W.I.
ONLY ADDRESS

Advert for Maison Georges, *Illustrated London News*, December 1934.

This important season, let French of London care for your hair. Let him create for you a look that's casual but cared for, 'easy' but elegant . . . let French dress your hair in a manner that's personal as your signature, but entirely sympathetic to the fashions of today.

French
OF LONDON

4 Curzon Place,   Park Lane, W.1. Grosvenor 3770-3778-3779

Advert for French of London, *The Queen*, June 1953.

heiress
to beauty...

from mother to daughter,
generation to generation,
Steiner has become
a living legend of elegance,
offering service and fashion
as contemporary as the hour.

S.P. All part of the Steiner Plan for more beautiful hair

Steiner HAUTE COIFFURE · BEAUTÉ

66 GROSVENOR STREET, LONDON, W.1. MAYFAIR 5345

LEICESTER, LEICESTER 27404   MANCHESTER, CENTRAL 7553   BIRMINGHAM, MIDLAND 7242
GLASGOW, CENTRAL 3584   LONDON AIRPORT, SKYPORT 1288   GLENEAGLES HOTEL,

THE QUEEN, MAY 11, 1960

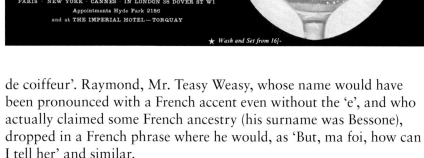

Sophisticated as champagne

the hair style with
a French accent
by

Antoine

PARIS · NEW YORK · CANNES · IN LONDON 38 DOVER ST W1
Appointments Hyde Park 2186
and at THE IMPERIAL HOTEL — TORQUAY

★ *Wash and Set from 16/-*

Above: Steiner, 'Haute Coiffure Beauté', *The Queen*, May 1960.

Above right: Antoine advert, 'Sophisticated as champagne', *The Tatler*, May 1960.

de coiffeur'. Raymond, Mr. Teasy Weasy, whose name would have been pronounced with a French accent even without the 'e', and who actually claimed some French ancestry (his surname was Bessone), dropped in a French phrase where he would, as 'But, ma foi, how can I tell her' and similar.

Not only did these brand stylists, many with chains of salons spreading from Mayfair to the suburbs and beyond, build their status by placing their advertisements in the most up-market publications, as *The Queen*, *The Tatler*, *Vogue* and *The Illustrated London News*, but hyped themselves as 'artists', not mere mortals who cut and groomed hair. Riche and Raymond tended to have photographs of themselves

Above: 'Raymond says' advert for Raymond, *The Tatler*, May 1960.

Opposite page: 'Riché is thinking of you', Riché advert, *The Queen*, February 1955.

in their advertisements, heads on hands, as if to portray themselves as serious thinkers. Raymond described himself as having 'the distinctive touch of the artist' producing exquisite results with 'a flick of inspiration'. Riche felt he had 'a mind like a jungle' – 'his is the most fertile imagination in the world of coiffure'. When Helena Rubinstein added hairstyling to her beauty salons, she referred to her stylists as 'master craftsmen'. Of course most of these hairdressers, these brand stylists, were publicity seekers, Antoine dressing himself in a white satin frock coat with silver nail varnish, Raymond in open sandals with painted toe nails.

When it came to hair products shampoo was one of the earliest to be advertised. Washing one's hair would have seemed curious to many Victorian women, even considered potentially harmful to one's health. Dirt was removed by endless brushing and towards the end of the century by dry shampooing, powder dusted on to the hair. Such powders, and early washing shampoos, were largely soap based, as Wrights Coal Tar Shampoo powder. It was not until 1927 that the German, Hans Schwarzkopf launched a liquid shampoo, and not until the mid-1930s that the American soap manufacturer, Procter & Gamble produced a synthetic shampoo, Drene.

Amani, manufactured by the British company Pritchard & Constance, was already well established in the 1920s, initially as a dry shampoo, for men and children as well as women. Early advertisements featured the results of the company's many publicity competitions, and also large photographs of stage personalities of

Riché *is thinking of you*

Riché has a mind like a jungle. His is the most fertile imagination in the world of coiffure.

You are the subject of his elegant fantasies. You whom he has, perhaps, seen passing that morning in Hay Hill. You for whom he now longs to create a coiffure of art.

You must call at his Hay Hill salon. Silence and efficiency reign (rather pleasant, this). Ask about his new "Lastic Lustre". Whatever you choose you will have all the wicked pleasure of *feeling* extravagant—while spending very much less than you expected. A shampoo and setting, for example, may be as little as 16/6. *Et quel chef d'œuvre de coiffure!*

RICHÉ FOR HAIR PERFECTION
14 Hay Hill, Berkeley Square, London, W.1
Telephone: HYDe Park 3368 (3 lines)

TRY RICHÉ PREPARATIONS AT HOME. GOOD STORES HAVE THEM — OR WILL ORDER THEM ESPECIALLY FOR YOU.

THE QUEEN, FEBRUARY 9, 1955

Above: 'The Shampoo of the Stars', Drene advert, *Housewife*, March 1947.

Opposite page: Various adverts for Amami, from left to right, *Good Housekeeping*, 1925; *Miss Modern*, October 1936; and *Housewife*, January 1944.

the day, as Phyllis Dare and Peggy Lamond, taken by the celebrity photographer Howard Carter. The shampoos were numbered 'specially blended for every shade and condition of hair'. By the 1930s Amami advertisements were boasting that these numbers had been 'scientifically graded' and the shampoos made from 'forty seven natural ingredients'. The tag 'Friday night is Amami night' maintained its popularity through to the 1950s and beyond.

An inter-war competitor for Amami was Silvikrin, again marketed to both men and women and similarly hyping its production being based on 'researches of famous scientists', but hardly matching the number of ingredients, a mere fourteen! By the onset of WWII the market was awash, as it were, with shampoos, the main players being Amami, Dreen, Evan Williams, Icilma, Silvikrin and Chesebrough's Vaseline Liquid Shampoo; Sunsilk, from Unilever, not entering the fray until the 1950s, Head and Shoulders, from Procter & Gamble launched in 1961. And when it came to conditioners Schwarzkopf was the first to launch a branded one, only to be overtaken by Alberto VO5 which was to gobble up nearly half the market.

Some shampoos, as Head & Shoulders and Sebbix, focused their advertising on the condition of the scalp, but most others on the hair itself using such threatening adjectives as 'dull', 'greasy', 'dry' and 'lifeless'. All emphasized cleanliness, even 'deep' cleanliness, Vaseline Liquid Shampoo actually 'floating out the dirt' , but also was added the effect of the shampoo on the surface, as well as on the roots, leaving the hair 'shining', 'sparkling' and with 'a silken sheen'.

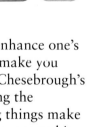
The line that by using a particular shampoo one could enhance one's beauty, come to look like stars of stage and screen, and make you attractive to whoever you wished, was used repeatedly. Chesebrough's Silken Sheen, in the 1950s was one such example assuring the potential user: 'your silky shining hair – these endearing things make him long to see you again and again.' Bristow's Lanolin suggested its own product will 'get the party spirit into your hair' and make you 'party bright, party pretty'.

After the hair was shampooed and dried, further products came to be considered essential, adding to the sheen, and keeping the hair in place. Chesebrough, early in the century had developed a pomade Vaseline to dress the hair, and, later, Hi-Lite served a similar

... or a hair type that's all your own

Max Factor know-how
made Sof-set hair spray
to take care of your hair

6/10

Sof·set
by MAX FACTOR

... and for your hair-piece too

The Benefits of Skilful
Hair Colouring

IGNORANCE of the possibilities of skilful Hair Colouring has prevented many a man and woman from benefiting from the discoveries of science regarding this important subject.

IF you are amongst the number, we would count it a pleasure to give you, in an interview or by letter, information which we have already conveyed to hundreds, to their lasting benefit and pleasure.

WE have studied the science of Hair Colouring thoroughly, and we are continually adding to our accumulated knowledge by daily practical experience. Consultations free.

J. Stewart Ltd

Hair Specialists & Wigmakers,

80, New Bond Street,
(Tel. 1711 Mayfair).

228, Regent Street,
(Tel. 5701 Mayfair).

LONDON, W.1.

Also at Glasgow, Edinburgh, Dundee.

Opposite page, left and centre:
Silvikrin Liquid Shampoo,
Woman's Realm, May 1958;
and Silvikrin 'Does Grow Hair',
Picture Post, November 1939.

Opposite page, right: Sunsilk,
Woman's Realm, 1964.

Above: Sof-set by Max Factor,
Vogue, February 1967.

Above right: J. Stewart Hair
Specialists & Wigmakers,
The Sketch, 1922.

purpose. But the breakthrough came in the post-WWII years and was a result of wartime activity. For insecticides for warfare on the Pacific front aerosols had been developed and aerosol hairsprays arrived on the market in the 1950s and '60s – so essential for the popular 'beehive', 'bouffant' and backcombing of the time. By the 1970s, 'is she... isn't she?', advertising Elida's Harmony Hairspray had become common parlance.

When it comes to hair dyeing, the lineage can practically be traced back to pre-history. Although examples, as the Celts going, was rather more to scare off the enemy than for any beautifying, the main motive became to resist ageing when hair colour faded and went grey. Generally people resorted to plant sources for dyes and it was not until

Paris creates a boon

For Women who dislike Grey Hair!

Here is wonderful news for women who have their hair tinted and for all those who dislike the idea of going grey. A revolutionary new hair tint, Imedia Creme 'D' from the famous hair research laboratories of L'Oreal, Paris, is now available here.

In one quick simple application, without pre-bleaching, Imedia Creme 'D' gently transforms grey hair to the soft,

staining, natural colour-beauty that you enjoyed at twenty. Your hair will be greyfree, beautiful, in your own natural colour—admired wherever you go—and no doubt envied.

But only Imedia Creme 'D' gives results like this. Insist on seeing the blue and gold tube of Imedia Creme 'D' *before* your hairdresser begins the tint.

You ask your hairdresser to use . . .
IMEDIA Creme 'D'
BY L'OREAL, PARIS
Made in twenty-seven subtle shades . . . Does not affect permanent waving.

Opposite page, left: Helena Rubinstein's Colour-Tint Rinses, *Vogue*, 1952.

Opposite page, right: Hiltone Bleach, *Homes & Gardens*, July 1946.

Above: Imedia Creme 'D', *The Queen*, February 1955.

the mid-nineteenth century when an English chemist, William Perkin, mistakenly stumbled on a mauve dye (when researching a cure for malaria), and not until the turn of the century when a French chemist, Eugène Schueller, launched Auriole (which was to become Oréale), that synthetic hair dyes came to the market.

Dyeing one's hair in Victorian times was as disreputable as wearing make-up, and the custom only seems to have been adopted by the masses from the 1920s. Anita Loos wrote *Gentlemen Prefer Blondes* in 1925, but this did not seem to have had such an immediate impact as Howard Hughes film *Platinum Blonde*, released in 1931, starring the blonde Jean Harlow. Generations of film stars were to help to maintain the desirability of being blonde – Mae West and Carol Lombard in the 1930s, Betty Grable and Veronica Lake in the '40s, Doris Day and Marilyn Monroe from the 1950s – and then came Brigitte Bardot. Dark hair stars just could not compete when it came to hair colour, even the glamorous Ava Gardner, Dorothy Lamour and Jane Russell or redheads, as Rita Hayworth. By the time of the staging and then filming of *Gentlemen Prefer Blondes*, in 1949 and 1953, and with the arrival of the first Barbie doll in 1959, blonde was the colour to be.

This did not stop manufacturers producing a range of dye colours. By the early 1950s Helena Rubinstein was offering '7 sensational colours' which she referred to as tints, as being rather more refined – tawny brown, dark brown, black satin, blue vixen, blonde Venus, copper leaf and corn silk Steiner, altogether less

Here I am
and I'm a blonde.
Blonde as sunshine
and I just want to
burst out laughing. And,
all because I used Hiltone,
everything's happening
and I feel like
taking off.

hiltone

It's a blonde's life!
Thanks! hiltone

'It's a blonde's life!', Hiltone
advert, *Vogue*, June 1969.

restrained, by 1953 was marketing gold, pink, blue, copper, lilac and silver. But L'Oréal was to top the lot with its Imedia in the mid-1950s – 27 shades – able to 'take the purchaser back to the colour they enjoyed at 20'. Eventually L'é was to be even sharper in its range when, in 1967, it targeted the woman who didn't mind being grey, in fact was prepared to flaunt it and make it fashionable; Grey Charm was hyped in advertisements with such copy as: 'Suddenly – you'll see what grey does for your eyes, your skin, your sparkle!' Not only was grey suggested as being an attractive colour but the customer was offered four grades – smoke grey, grey mink, opal grey and muted silver.

Initially advertising of hair dye stressed its scientific origin and, consequently, that only professionals could know how to handle it. An advertisement appearing in *The Sketch* in 1922 from Stewart's of Bond Street was typical:

Ignorance of the possibilities of skillful hair colouring has prevented many a man and woman from benefiting from the discoveries regarding this important new subject.

L'Oréal with Imedia advertised its dye as coming from 'the famous research laboratories in Paris'; Rubinstein, as was her wont, had her Colour-Tint Rinses develop by the 'cosmetic scientist Helena Rubinstein'. And indeed customers needed such reassurance for many of these early dye products could well have harmful effects if misused.

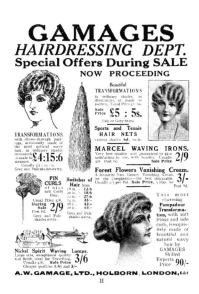

Although hair dyeing continued to be a service offered by salons with specially trained staff, frequently allotted a discrete space in the salon to avoid other customers knowing what was going on, eventually dyes came on the market that could be brought easily for home use. Schwarzkopf claimed the first home hair colourant with its Poly Colour in 1947. By the 1950s the husband and wife team Lawrence Gelb and Jane Clair had launched Miss Clairol Hair Colour Bath, a home dyeing kit. Its accompanying advertising campaign with copywriter Shirley Polykoff, made 'Does she or doesn't she?' the tag of the time. Home colouring became a norm.

Dyeing as something disreputable, to be carried out secretly, was to morph into something acceptable, even fashionable, following the hair colours of the celebrities of the moment, and eventually something done for sheer fun or even an art form. By the late 1960s 'Hiltone' advertisements carried such copy as 'I just wanted to burst out laughing' and 'I feel like taking off'. By the time Vivienne Westwood's punk style crashed the fashion world in the 1970s, dyeing did become a sort of art form – highlighting, lowlighting, root touch-ups, block colouring – in any colour or colour combination it became a matter of personal choice, of personal adventuring. Dyeing was no longer a matter of shame, but, as L'Oréal would have it – 'Because you're worth it'.

Along with the actual products rubbed in, washed, sprayed, applied to the hair to beautify it were the various bits and bobs to keep hair in place as well as hand held articles to brush and dry it. With the elaborate hair styles of the Victorians and Edwardians, with much folding, piling, swirling of long tresses, came articles for padding, means of fixing it all, of keeping everything in place. In addition there would be 'extras to affix, from single ringlets and partial 'vistors' to full wigs, all of which were widely advertised to look 'natural', and had the backing of being 'artistically designed'. Hair pins, of one kind or another, had been used throughout history, but the breed of pin that was to dominate the twentieth century market, the one that was advertised most widely, was Kirbigrip, manufactured by Kirby Beard of Birmingham. These pins were sold

The Queen of Hair Brushes

A Mason Pearson brush is incomparable for promoting healthy hair—and healthy hair is one of the greatest assets a woman can possess. It takes a permanent wave better, *keeps a permanent wave longer,* and sets more easily and charmingly.

Regular brushing with a Mason Pearson will keep *your* hair in radiant condition. With its slender spired tufts of nylon or black wild boar bristle, set in a pneumatic rubber cushion, the Mason Pearson penetrates right to the scalp. Lifting every disarranged strand into place, it restores the set to its proper formation. You can *feel* it stimulating . . . aerating . . . sweeping away dust and dandruff!

And remember, a Mason Pearson improves a permanent wave. Ask at your chemist's, hairdresser's or stores.

POCKET SIZE
10/-
SHINGLE
13/10
GENTLE
16/2
AND OTHERS UP TO 52/6

Write to Mason Pearson Bros., 70 Piccadilly London, W.1, for attractive post free booklet.

MASON PEARSON
London   England

For over 150 years

Hindes HAIR BRUSHES

HAVE BEEN FAMOUS FOR QUALITY

Every brush beautifully made by Master Craftsmen. Superior finish, long lasting wear. Rubber cushion brushes

Ask for a Hindes HAIR BRUSH and get the best

Prices ranging from 4/3 to 29/9

HINDES LIMITED, BROMSGROVE ST., BIRMINGHAM 5

Heady as the tang
     of an autumn bonfire—

— the lively thrill of
     this astonishing new

HALEX Combing Brush

158 firm but resilient plastic quills
slide through even the deepest, heaviest
locks—give gentle friction and tonic
exercise to the hair-roots and the head.

as 'scientific' and as able to secure 'even the shortest locks', 'never fall out', and 'snuggle in the hair'. They came in black or bronze and were 'available everywhere'.

One way of ensuring shiny hair, whether long or short, was brushing it, yet again, traceable back to early civilisations. Kent always claimed itself to be the oldest British company producing brushes, founded in 1777, just pipping Hindes, a Birmingham manufacturer. A later competitor was Mason Pearson, bringing its cushioned brush to the market in 1885 to be followed by Halex.

Opposite page: Advert for Halex, *Housewife*, December, 1948.

Above: Allure Perfume Hairbrush, *Homes & Gardens*, July 1946.

The advertising of hairbrushes tended to emphasise the quality of construction as much, if not more, than their contribution to the beautifying of tresses. Much was made of Britishness, of the rarity of the bristles ('genuine Siberian boar'), of the wood of the handles ('finest satinwood'), and frequently that the whole product came from the hands of 'skilled craftsmen'. Kent and Hindes competed for ancestry, Kent winning by some twenty years, and Kent was inclined to mention that amongst its buyers were 'Royalty of Europe and the culture public'. Tradition was everything when it came to advertising brushes, effect was often an afterthought.

Mason Pearson did occasionally let its hair down, as it were, as with an advertisement in *The Queen* in the 1950s assuring users that the effect of brushing with its products would be: 'stimulating – aerating… sweeping away dust and dandruff'

Sexual attraction was very rarely used, at least in the years covered by this book, although Kent, by then Kent-Cosby, in a wartime advertisement, did go as far as saying that their brushes 'brush beauty and fragrance into your hair' when it offered a perfumed pad under the brittle pad, even branding the specimen 'Allure'.

For those with straight hair, when curls and waves were in fashion, extra accessories and equipment were needed. A damp tress could, temporarily be made to curl by wrapping it round one's finger and pinning it in place with a grip or curling paper. Hair could been made more lastingly wavy when, at the end of the eighteenth century, François Marcel introduced his curling tongs, hair to be wrapped

Permanently Waved by

EUGÈNE

THE above photograph is entirely typical of the work being done at Eugène's **Headquarters** in Grafton Street. You will agree that it answers every question as to whether permanently waved hair can be as beautiful as naturally wavy hair. We are able to achieve these results widely because the Eugène Waving Apparatus is the most scientifically accurate existing, and because we employ only **highly skilled operators.** We don't ask you to believe this off-hand—much harm has already been done to permanent waving by the exaggerated claims of people practising with obsolete machines and unskilled knowledge. We ask you to come and prove with your own eyes where our process differs from all others.

OUR patrons, who have come every six months to have their newly grown hair waved, **know** that we achieve every claim we make—that we **can** permanently wave hair in exact reproduction of the most beautiful natural wave, and **without harming the hair.** No unbecoming frizz or brittleness accompanies the Eugène permanent wave—the wave is soft and lasting—the newly grown hair can be waved after six months or more **without** affecting the part previously treated. **We guarantee this,** and if the hair is unsuitable for permanent waving, we do not undertake it. **Before** you have your hair waved we invite you to our unique film demonstration at 23, Grafton Street. Here, on living models, you can see the whole process of Eugène Permanent Waving. An expert is in attendance to explain or give advice on any question relating to the hair. Displayed **free** to every enquirer.

It is essential to have specially trained operators for waving "bobbed" hair. We have them.

SEND TO-DAY
for our new booklet. It is beautifully illustrated, and contains the whole story of Permanent Waving. You will find it most interesting and convincing. Please ask for 6th edition.

EUGÈNE
Inventor and Patentee of the world-famous Eugène hair-waving appliances.
**23, GRAFTON STREET,
LONDON, W.1.**
(Approached from Dover St. or Old Bond St.)
Telephone : Gerrard 6487.
EUGÈNE & CO.,   EUGÈNE LTD.,
10, King Street,   265, Rue St. Honoré,
MANCHESTER.   PARIS.

SETAGÈNE
is a setting lotion for permanently waved and naturally wavy hair. It is not only its effectiveness in setting a soft and becoming wave in the hair which has won it such enthusiastic praise from our patrons—it is the gorgeous sheen and lustre this lotion imparts to the hair, and for scalp massage its tonic qualities are invaluable.

PRICES : 2/6 per bottle, with fine spray attached 10/6. Larger size 10/6; with spray 15/6. Postage paid.

Above: 'Permanently Waved by Eugéne', *The Sketch*, 1922.

Right: Eugéne's simplified approach, *Housewife*, June 1944.

EUGÈNE

★ **P**rove this new
machineless permanent
wave on your own hair

NO WIRES
NO HEATERS
NO ELECTRICITY

Here at last
is perfect permanent
waving without para-
phernalia. Jamal leaves you utterly
free, free to walk about, read or phone
your friends during the process. The
featherlight Jamal vapet takes the place
of wires, heaters and electricity, and with
the Jamalotion graded specially for your
hair conjures deep lasting waves and soft
springy curls.

LEADING HAIRDRESSERS
SPECIALIZE IN JAMAL

Thousands of leading hairdressers are
Jamal enthusiasts. It enables them to get
splendid results on all types and textures
of hair, and to achieve all the lovely
modern styles. Ask one of them to prove
what Jamal will do to make your hair
more lovely.

★ **Jamal specialists will**
give you a free proof curl
if necessary

How Jamal gives you a
perfect perm without wires,
heaters or electricity

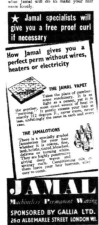

THE JAMAL VAPET
Takes the place of cumber-
some machinery. It is as
light as a penny, yet it is
the gentlest, most exact source of heat in
"perming." It gently steams your hair at
exactly 212 degrees F., never more, never
less, unfailingly the same in each and every
case.

THE JAMALOTIONS
There is a specially graded
Jamalotion for your hair
whether it is coarse, fine,
lank, brittle, tinted, bleached,
delicate or turning white.
They are highly penetrating
giving deep waves and
springy curls. Conditioning oils in
them leave your hair lustrous, silky,
easy to comb.

JAMAL
Machineless Permanent Waving

SPONSORED BY GALLIA LTD.
26a ALBEMARLE STREET LONDON W.1.

around the blunt edge, an advance on heating a pair of scissors. Marcel waving irons were still being sold by department stores, as Gamages, well into the 1920s.

But Marcel waving tongs were to be overtaken by the Eugene Waving Apparatus. Karl Nessler, a German, who took the French name Nestle on moving to London in 1901, already was advocating electrically heated rods for attaining waves, but the Eugene brand was to swamp the market with its own technique. An advertisement in *The Sketch* in 1922 hyped it as 'the most scientifically accurate existing' used only by 'skilled operators', with results lasting six months. And, to reassure the customer, nervous that electricity was to be used, explained that the whole process could be seen on film before hand. Advertisements for Eugene morphed from early ones with copious copy explaining the process in detail, to ones bearing a balance of photography and copy. By the 1940s, such was its dominance, that it was sufficient for an advertisement merely to be a photograph of the finished work of art with the word Eugene in large font, at the bottom.

But then came the machine-less permanent waving products – the 'cold wave' – as Lustrom and Jamal – 'no wires, no heaters, no electricity'; and to become market leader Toni, which unlike the first two which were applied by salon professionals, could be used at home. It was the idea of the American ad-man Daniel J. Edelman, in the early 1950s, to use twins with the caption 'which twin has the Toni' – which twin had an expensive salon perm and which twin had a Toni

Above: 'Who's her Hairdresser?',
Jamal, *Vogue*, June 1953.

Right: 'Which Twin has the Toni?',
Punch, April 1949.

A G.E.C. PRODUCT

"MAGNET"
ELECTRIC HAIR DRYER

An elegant appearance demands constant attention to your hair. Enjoy an invigorating toilet without effort by using the MAGNET Electric Hair Dryer. Not only does it do its job thoroughly well, but, being made of reinforced fabric Bakelite (mottled brown), it possesses great strength and will not crack or break with ordinary care. This high-class product costs only 39/6—if supplied with antique copper stand (for the table or adjustable as a wall-bracket), 8/6 extra.

WRITE to address below for folder HA6998P, which gives particulars of the complete range of G.E.C. Household Electric Appliances— sent Post-Free on request.

G.E.C. BRITISH MADE QUALITY PRODUCTS

THE GENERAL ELECTRIC CO., LTD. *Head Office and Public Showrooms: Magnet House, Kingsway, London, W.C.2 Branches throughout Great Britain and in all principal markets of the world.*

A GIFT OF
Lasting Pleasure

Whether you hope to receive a gift or plan to give one, your choice should provide lasting pleasure.

Here are two superb ideas for gifts that are not only elegant in themselves, but impart beauty and good health to the lucky recipients.

PIFCO ELECTRIC VIBRATORY *Massager*

★ Pifco Vibratory Massager... 88/5d.
Pifco Streamlined Hairdryer... 93/11d.

A de luxe carrying case now available for both Hairdryer and Massager.

Obtainable at good-class Chemists, Electricians and Stores. Write for illustrated folders and name of nearest stockist to: Pifco Ltd., Watling Street, Manchester, 4.

PIFCO STREAMLINED *Hair Dryer*

Above: Magnet Electric Hair Dryer, G.E.C., *Punch*, June 1935.

Above right: 'A Gift of Lasting Pleasure', Pifco Streamlined Hair Dryer, *Vogue*, December 1952.

do-it-yourself kit, that caught the imagination of the public and helped make the product a winner.

That women could style their own hair at home was further aided by the arrival of the home hair drier, largely a spin-off from the manufacturers of electrical goods. G.E.C. had already marketed its Magnet in the 1930s, and the 'streamline' PIFCO was launched in the 1950s. Philips was to build up a whole Beauty Care department, which came to include not only driers but straighteners. Whatever the fashion women could now make their own decisions – what to do themselves, and what to leave to the salon professionals.

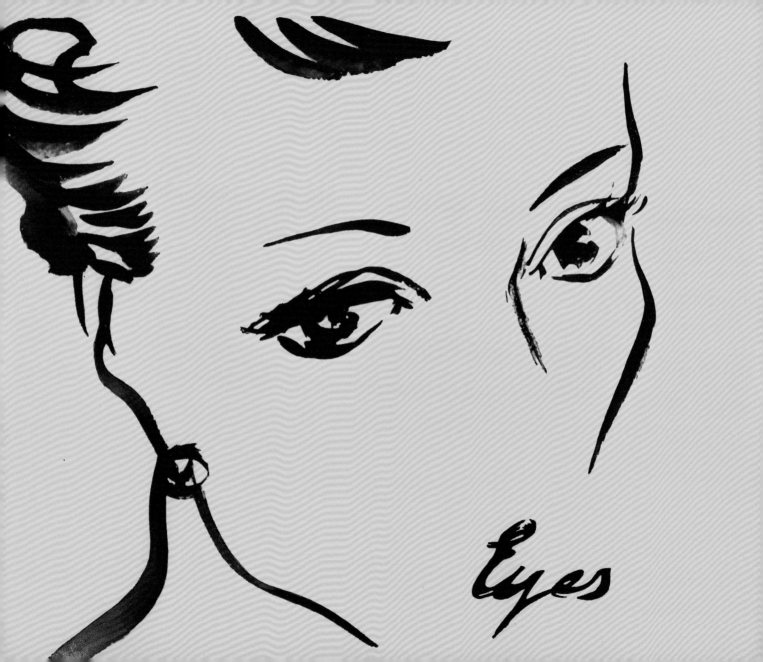

Eyes

Eyes

'When a woman isn't beautiful people always say "You have lovely eyes".'

Uncle Vanya, Chekhov

Given that the eyes and eyebrows are considered key to someone communicating feelings, for centuries they received little attention when it came to enhancement by make-up. Much is made of the Egyptians paying homage to Horus, the sky god, whose decorated eye was believed to be a symbol for protection and good health. Archaeologists have found evidence of eye make-up not only in the tombs of pharaohs but in those of ordinary citizens. Egyptians made their eyes more pronounced by darkening, arching and elongating their eyebrows. The Greeks, however, generally let their eyebrows be, particularly if they met in the middle – a sign of wisdom. Fast forward to the Middle Ages, and onto to Elizabethan times, when eyebrows were plucked or removed completely – and then silence.

It appears that eye-brows, that can so emphasise meaning, were largely neglected, really until after WWI when, with the coming of the silent film, every aspect of the face needed attention in order to communicate, and cinema goers aped the stars. When Greta Garbo, in the 1930s, completely plucked her brows, penciling in great crescent-

'Beautify your Lashes', Maybelline,
Miss Modern, October 1936.

shaped sweeps, eyebrow brushes, shades and pencils arrived on the market. Eyebrows thickened again with Lauren Bacall's natural look and then demanded shaping following the lush brows of Elizabeth Taylor and Audrey Hepburn. Rimmel produced an Eye-Beauty pencil for defining eyebrows, whatever the fashion; whilst Revlon, in the 1960s, was actually advising what was considered to be the shape of the time with a brow powder to be applied with a special-angled brush to arch and then taper off – any excess hairs below the brow to be tweezed out.

Products to enhance eyelashes were on sale before the turn of the century albeit there is some doubt about Rimmel's claim to have originated mascara, as its Superfin is now thought to have been initially for moustaches rather than lashes. Sold in cake form in a small cardboard or metal box with a mirror and tiny brush, early mascara was much used in the theatre before turning to the mass market. Rimmel, initially, marketed by mail order and by the placement of advertisements in special publications, as theatre programmes.

It is generally accepted that the first mass-marketed mascara was developed by an Illinois chemist, T.L. Williams, in 1917, for his sister Mabel, who took responsibility for its popularization, her name contributing to its brand name – Maybeline. Maybeline, as Superfin was sold in cake form and applied by spit and brush, not the easiest form for accurate application, albeit an improvement from earlier homemade products applied by fingers dusted with coal dust and the like.

EYE LOVELINESS

LALEEK Longlash brings out the beauty of the eyes and gives glamour and depth to their expression. Longlash strengthens and darkens as it grows lovely lashes. Start to use Longlash to-day and watch your eyes grow in allure. In four shades :—Midnight Blue, Copper Beech, Raven Black and Colourless 1/-. Special Brush 4d.

At all Stores, Boots, and good chemists.

Adelaide Grey

27, OLD BOND ST., LONDON, W.1.

Above: 'Eye Loveliness', Adelaide Grey, *Home Notes*, June 1940.

Right: Eylure Real Hair Lashes, *Vogue*, June 1969.

EYES RIGHT ANY WOMAN WHO...

wishes there were lashes to make close-set eyes look wide apart...or little deep-set eyes look wide-eyed and wonderful...or lashes made specially for girls who wear glasses. Eyes right any woman who doesn't know that only Eylure make over 30 different styles and that you can try them before you actually have a flutter!

NOW MORE AND MORE exciting lashes from Eylure

SUPER-DOOPER lashes with Under-lashes

Sable Style

YOU'RE SURE THEY'RE PURE-THEY'RE EYLURE
-every box sealed for your protection

Left: Miners Real Hair Lashes, *Woman's Own*, November 1969.

Above: 'Eye-Matched Makeup keyed to the colour of your Eyes', Richard Hudnut, *Miss Modern*, October 1936.

By the 1920s and into the '30s it became acceptable to have lashes that were noticeable. Adeline Grey in advertising its mascara warned:

> If your lashes are short, rough and uneven the allure is lost.

And Maybeline advertisements were even fiercer:

> Pale scanty lashes simply will not do. Fashion decrees that they must appear naturally long, dark, luxuriant, sweeping.

Crescent reassuring:

> The secret of lovely lashes that add charm and personality to the plainest features.

The main concerns when using mascara were that it could be applied accurately, that it did not smudge, that it was not affected by water and that it wasn't harmful to ones health. By the 1930s Maybeline was promising all of this: 'non-smarting, tearproof, harmless and darkening'. Even into the 1950s Helena Rubinstein was still finding it necessary to tell its buyers of mascara that 'it wouldn't smear, streak or run', when she sold her latest version – a cream in a tube.

As with other make-up products, mascara came to be linked with fashion, users being advised that they should match colour of eyelashes to colours of clothes. Maybeline was one of the first making the link with its Eyelash Beautifier in 1929. Colours began to be added to the original black. An Adeline Gray advertisement for its mascara in the 1930s offered, in addition to raven black, midnight blue, copper beech and colourless. Elizabeth Arden added green and violet to the standard range, Helena Rubinstein grey. Although tearproof was assured in many pre-war mascara advertisements, this became a major selling aspect in the post-war years when Maybeline introduced what was to become a best-seller – Ultra Lash.

Those with the abhorrent 'short' or 'scanty' lashes could always resort to adding on false ones. These became popular with the arrival of the movies, when 'close-ups' would reveal any deficiencies. Charles Nestle, a German, who was to introduce the permanent wave, invented a machine that made false lashes, which he sold from his New York hairdressers. It is said that W.G. Griffiths experimented with having his stars use false lashes when he was making *Intolerance*; and Max Factor, who worked closely with the studios, offered 'fashion lashes' amongst his product range.

False lashes were not widely advertised until after WWII, with Miner's 'real hair' lashes and Eylure. Luscious lashes were hyped not merely to make up for deficiencies, but for experimentation, for fun. In addition to Eylure's adage 'You're sure they're pure they're Eylure' it, as well as Maybeline, gave lashes fun, even sexy, names as Miner's 'natty', 'flashy', 'flighty' and 'wild and wicked' and Eylure's 'whopper' and 'coquette'. Twiggy was to paint on lower lashes, and lashes came to be

The Mykonos Look

It puts the sunlit Aegean into your eyes.

This is the Greek Islands year.

(As if you didn't know.) And Helena Rubinstein has the fashion for it. Marvelous cool-lucre elegance. Rich, but unbrazen. You get it with our new Illumination Eye Make-Up. In fantastically clear, unadulterated colours.

From that most vivifying sun-washed Greek Island: Mykonos.

Sorceress eyes: Bold sweeps of Aegean Blue. Golden Lime. Earthy Brown. And the Alabaster White of Greek statues.

Roseate lips like wild pink island flowers with Sunlight Pink Lipstick.

Wear the Mykonos Look to Greece on Olympic Airways.

It's the newest look in aeons. Makes you look the way you feel after a splash in the Aegean.

From the complete Mykonos collection: consider this eye-deal trio. Fluid eyeliner. Creme eyeshadow. Waterproof mascara.

Illumination Eye Make-Up by Helena Rubinstein

Left: The Mykonos Look, Helena Rubinstein, *Vogue*, June 1969.

Above: 'Glamorise your eyes with Rimmel', *Vanity Fair*, October 1956.

Right: 'To put the stars in your eyes', Max Factor, *Vanity Fair*, October 1956.

Far right: Elizabeth Arden advertisement, *c.* 1937.

offered as 'lower' as well as 'upper', and, in fact, eventually every need seems to have been adequately met with Eylure's 'thirty different styles'.

Eye shadow was a product slower to take off in spite of Elizabeth Arden and Max Factor both producing early versions, said to be inspired by the flamboyant colours of Diaghilev's touring Ballet Russes. Decades later Yves St. Laurent was actually to offer a range of eye shadow named Ballets Russe. Again it was the cinema that kick-started the mass popularity of eye shadow, particularly, in the post-war years with Elizabeth Taylor's heavily lidded eye make up for her role as Cleopatra, spurring the likes of Revlon to produce an entire Egyptian line.

When it came to eye shadow colour, Maybeline started fairly conservatively offering blue, brown, black and green; by the 1930s Elizabeth Arden advertised a range of fifteen colours; Helena Rubinstein although outdone in numbers added the refinement of white – 'the alabaster white of Greek statues'. In the post-war years even more colours were achievable when firms suggested combining colours as Coty's with 'Pick and Paint'. Eye shadow came to be sold not only in boxes containing a single colour but in multi-colours, some boxes extending to fifty colours or more.

From the 1930s the major beauty product companies began to offer more than one eye make-up preparation, many offering the whole range. A Richard Hudnutt advertisement in Miss Modern of 1936 had on offer just mascara and eye shadow; when, at about the same time, Elizabeth Arden was outdoing the whole field with her Venetian Special Eye Cream, Puffy-Eye strap, Venetian Eyelash Grower, Venetian Eyelash Cosmetique and Ardena Eye-Shadow. But it was Mary Quant who would suggest that making up one's eyes was not a weighty matter but could be fun, with her liquid shadow, eye shapers, cake liner, eye liner, eye pencil, black and liquid mascara – all in off-beat colours; pre-war timidity morphed into 60s outrageous when Yardley's, not to be outdone, focused on Twiggy's eyes to sell its products, the eyes dominating the whole advertising space.

Lips & Nails

'My mother warned me to avoid things coloured red.'

Claes Oldenburg

'Innate releasing mechanisms' was a term coined by human and animal behaviorists to suggest that certain external stimuli produce, invariably, the same innate responses – a kind of hardwiring to the brain. Although it is clear that a good deal of human behaviour is a matter of culture and custom rather than instinct, there is something about the colour red, particularly when applied to lips and nails, that tempts one to feel that something very basic, if not actually instinctual, is going on between the porter of the red touches and the invariably stimulated viewer.

Although in earlier periods the reddening of lips and nails signified high status in Western societies, up to the twentieth century the obvious painting of lips and nails was generally unacceptable, in some way a threat to society, at the very least a sign of rebellion but more often one of immorality and decadence. That there was something intrinsically dangerous yet exciting in the use of red, even when painting lips and nails had become generally acceptable, is perhaps exemplified in the names given to many commercial lipsticks and nail varnishes – Guerlain's 'Rouge d'Enfers', Cutex's 'pink TNT', Innoxa's 'Fire Dance' and Chen Yu's 'Imperial Flame'.

In Western culture, nails were generally left natural or buffed to give a light shine until after WWI. Buffing was done with a slightly abrasive surface and most Victorian and Edwardian manicure sets would include a nail buffer covered in chamois leather to give the appropriate degree of friction. If used, nail varnish had to be imperceptible. Dr. J. Parker Pray advertised his Rosaline as a tint 'true to nature, not detected'.

It was just before WWI that a Connecticut manufacturer produced Cutex, generally considered one of the first nail 'tints'; and not until well after that war that its main rivals – Peggy Sage (founded 1925) and Revlon (founded 1932) arrived on the scene.

Peggy Sage aimed for a classy international brand image, centering its business in Paris, setting up a chain of international manicure salons, naming its varnishes along the lines 'Biarritz', 'Palm Beach' and 'Lido' and advertising in the smarter magazines as 'The Queen' and 'Harpers'. Peggy Sage, when seeking to develop, sought tie-ups with the likes of Coty, Lentheric and Charles of the Ritz. Its advertisements claimed its polishes 'the most luxurious ever created' and its nail varnish container 'the most beautiful in the world'.

Charles Revson of Revlon also hoped to give his products class, advertising that they were 'originated by a New York socialite'; (his girl friend was Dianne Vreeland's manicurist and he experimented with some varnish she had brought back from Europe). He named his

66

HANDLE WITH CARE...
IT'S LOADED WITH LOVELINESS!

"pink T.N.T."

Beautiful dynamite for your lips. Gay as fireworks! Exciting as a carnival!
"PINK T.N.T." is a radiant, rocketing new pink, sparked with a touch of blue.
Get "PINK T.N.T." today and start the new season off with a beautiful bang!

For lasting beauty   CUTEX *Stay Fast* lipstick

3250-2   OBTAINABLE FROM ALL CHEMISTS AND STORES

Left: Cutex Stay Fast lipstick,
Milady, August 1957.

Above: Yardley lipstick advert by
Coleman, Prentis & Varley, *c.* 1962.

One coat of Amami perfumed Nail Varnish will give you gleaming, sparkling nails—a smooth and even brilliance that lasts unspoilt for a week.
You will find that a 6d. Bottle will last for months.

IN 5 FASHIONABLE SHADES:—
Colourless,
Natural,
Coral,
Rose and
Ruby

6D.
per Bottle

To prepare your nails for the most perfect manicure, use Amami Nail Varnish Remover—oily and richly perfumed, in new large 6d. bottle. Also Amami Cuticle Remover, 6d.

Amami, *Miss Modern*,
October 1936.

varnish Revlon Nail Enamel as he considered 'enamel' a posher word than 'polish' and began his marketing through beauty salons. By 1937 he was selling through chemists and department stores as well. It was Revson who is acknowledged as bringing nail products to the masses. His image was, perhaps, always slightly tainted by the likes of such doyen as Rubinstein and Arden making clear that they considered him a vulgar upstart selling a vulgar product. Arden did not enter into the 'vulgar' nail business until 1940; although Rubinstein had ventured into that market slightly earlier.

Nail varnish came in a variety of forms – pastes, powders, blocks – before a liquid form was generally adopted. The criteria that might possibly distinguish different brands were how easily it could be applied, that it dried quickly, that it was long-lasting, that it did not chip, that it was fire-proof and that its container did not spill easily. Typical were the advertisements for Amami and Peggy Sage in the 1930s, with Amami claiming:

> One coat of Amami perfumed nail varnish will give you gleaming, sparkling nails – a smooth and even brilliance that lasts unspoilt for a week.

And Peggy Sage:

> Its clever jewel-like sparkle on your finger tips gleams longer than you would believe possible.

68

Peggy Sage, 'Nail polish with the
crystallin finish', *Milady*, June 1952.

Peggy Sage, '21 colours',
The Queen, June 1953.

Right: Guerlain, 'Automatic Lipstick', 1938.

Far right: Elizabeth Arden, 'Montezuma Red', by Coleman, Prentis & Varley, 1942.

Originally varnish was meant to be imperceptible but gradually colours were introduced. Cutex was especially slow in this respect having, in the 1930s only six on offer; by the 1950s Revlon had overtaken most of its rivals with some thirty-three. Revlon soon hit on the marketing strategy of bringing out new colours every spring and autumn chiming in with the 'fashion' seasons. Peggy Sage was to climb on this band wagon advertising her varnishes as being: 'a vast array of subtle couturier shades.'

But it was the linking of nail varnish colours with those of lipstick that extended the colour range further, as lipstick was well in advance when it came to colours and varnish felt obliged to catch up. Cutex advertising made the link early with its catchy: 'finger tips and lovely lips.'

If scarlet nails stirred animal instincts, how much greater was the impact of scarlet lips. Again examples of lip-painting have been traced to early civilisations, yet again occurring both in the upper and lower echelons of society. There are later examples of colouring ones lips, and Elizabeth I is said to have died with scarlet on her lips, glowing out from her over-whitened skin. But with the church's opposition the bulk of the female population was left to 'bite its lip' if a stronger colour was required.

Outdoor Girl, 'Lively lips match dresses', *Home Notes*, August 1939.

Cutex, 'Since colour is the point', *Woman*, February 1959.

New
L·I·V·E·L·Y
lips match
dresses ☆

Have a lively Outdoor Girl Lipstick to match every dress you wear! Everyone's doing it—ringing the changes on lips . . and Outdoor Girl's dress-matching lipsticks are l-i-v-e-l-y, l-o-v-e-l-y—with base of olive oil to nourish lip tissues, make them soft and gleaming, make colour come a-l-i-v-e on your lips. (Of course, Outdoor Girl Powder, Cream Rouge and Nail Gloss are blended to tone with Lipstick shades.)

WRITE TO-DAY *for our clever miniature lipstick set—four lively little Outdoor Girl Lipsticks matched to new dress colours. Send 4½d. in stamps to Crystal Products Ltd. (Dept. D. 37), Brunel Road, East Acton, W.3, and say if you are* FAIR, MEDIUM, *or* DARK, *or if you would like the new* BRONZED SUN TAN SET.

OUTDOOR GIRL
OLIVE OIL LIPSTICK
2/6, 1/-, 6d.
The Liveliest Lipstick in Town

since colour
is the point...

be sure
you pick
the lipstick
with more
colour in it

Be brilliant. Wear Cutex . . . the lipstick with richer, truer colour. *Dazzling* colour that LASTS hour after hour . . . smooth, lustrous, *vibrant.* Wear Cutex . . . the lipstick that *never* dries your lips—*always* keeps its fresh, first-on creaminess. Full size in a classic golden case, 2/9. 12 glowing colours to choose from.

CUTEX lipstick

Ideal Home

Hollywood's New fashion
in Lip Make-Up

Rita Hayworth
in "DOWN TO EARTH"
A Columbia Picture

A NEW rainbow of lipstick reds . . . to harmonize with every colouring . . . to blend with every costume . . . to match every mood.

★ The colour stays on until you take it off

★ New original formula does not dry the lips

★ New kind of lip make-up . . . oh! so s-m-o-o-t-h

THREE SHADES FOR YOUR TYPE
correct for your colouring . . .
correct for your costume

	CLEAR RED	BLUE RED	ROSE RED
BLONDES	CLEAR RED	BLUE RED No. 1	ROSE RED No. 1
BRUNETTES	CLEAR RED No. 3	BLUE RED No. 3	ROSE RED No. 3
BROWNETTES	CLEAR RED No. 2	BLUE RED No. 2	ROSE RED No. 2
REDHEADS	CLEAR RED No. 1	BLUE RED No. 1	ROSE RED No. 1

MAX FACTOR 'Cosmetics of the Stars' are obtainable from your local Chemist, Hairdresser & Store.

In a modern-design metal case

Max Factor HOLLYWOOD

NEW LIPSTICK COLOURS—NEW LOOK!

CORNALINE new triumph for BLONDES
BOIS de ROSE new perfection for BRUNETTES
CAROUBIER new success for REDHEADS
Rouge and Varnish to match

LANCÔME

Opposite page, right: Max Factor, 'Hollywood's New fashion in Lip Make-up', featuring Rita Hayworth, *Ideal Home*, November 1947.

Above right: Lancôme advert, 'New Lipstick Colours', *Tatler*, May 1960.

An early lipstick is said to have come from the perfume house Guerlain. When lipsticks came to be marketed they came wrapped in paper with a brush for application. However, it was not really until the 1920s that colouring one's lips became generally acceptable, and it was the Americans who devised clever containers to enable lipsticks to be carried easily in handbags, with metal cases that had a swivel mechanism for the stick to be revealed and withdrawn. And it was also an American, one Hazel Bishop, who, in the 1940s, developed a non-smear lipstick advertised to: 'stay on you, not on him'.

The way lipstick was applied was much influenced by Hollywood, both as to the outline of the shape (as with Clara Bow's cupid's bow) and the colour, as with the likes of Rita Heyworth and Elizabeth Taylor.

If advertising was eventually to give nail varnish a sexy slant, this was to be even more pronounced with the marketing of lipstick. As early as 1927 the French launched what was to be a best seller, a lipstick actually named 'Rouge Baiser', using one of the major commercial artists of the day, René Gruau, to produce iconic images for its advertisements.

At the cheaper end of the market, manufacturers were giving their lines suggestive names and exotic auras, as with a 1940s Tattoo advertisement copy:

> The gold-dusted South Sea maidens who know all lover's answers found the dawn-dewy secret that belongs to Tattoo.

And a rather more restrained example from Innoxa, in the 1960s: 'Innoxa didn't exactly invent romance. But they did a lot to promote it.' This presumably by lipsticks being named 'love letters', 'candy kisses' and the like.

Opposite page, left: Max Factor, *Housewife*, August 1948.

Opposite page, right: Tattoo, 'South Seas Shades', *Lilliput*, April 1949.

Above: Chen Yu Imperial Flame, *The Queen*, June 1953.

Right: Gala of London, *Modern Woman*, November 1949.

Above: Atkinsons Salon Tested Cosmetics, *Vogue*, June 1953.

Right: 'Revlon invents wet lipstick', *Vogue*, February 1967.

Revlon invents wet lipstick

Here's a beautiful new breed of lipstick. Lush. Liquidy. Mouth-watering. 'Moon Drops' *wet* lipstick makes dry lips a thing of the past. It's literally loaded with lustre, yet the texture is unbelievably light. *Wet* lipstick almost skims on. (Other lipsticks seem to drag on by comparison.) The feel is fantastic. Like wearing no lipstick at all. And the look is incredible.

'Moon Drops' lipstick   **invented by Revlon**

Above: Elizabeth Arden, 'Pink Perfection', *The Tatler*, June 1953.

By the onset of the Second World War many of the major beauty product manufacturers were selling both nail varnish and lipstick, usually having advertisements covering the two, as with Revlon and Peggy Sage. One of Revlon's launching of linked products in the 1950s is generally considered a master stroke, a campaign that stood out as iconic, by some considered brazen – 'Fire and Ice'. Revlon used the photographer Richard Avedon with the model dramatically clothed in a tight silver dress and draped in a scarlet fabric, showing colour-matching of lips and nails. The copy read: 'for you who love to flirt with fire… who dare to skate with thin ice…'.

This was accompanied by a somewhat bizarre questionnaire as to the reader's sexual habits, were they 'naughty or nice', with such questions as 'have you ever wanted to wear an ankle bracelet?', and, more directly, 'Do you close your eyes when you are kissed?'

Truth would out! Revlon blatantly revealed, and got accepted, that there was a sexual element to the use of lipstick and nail varnish, but gave a sophistication to the fact. Oldenburg's mother was, perhaps, wise to advise her son against the colour red, which certainly seems to serve as an innate releasing mechanism, not only attracting others, but, further, hinting at availability!

VEET

A CREAM THAT REMOVES HAIR.

Delicacies

Every woman who yearns to become more attractive faces their own personal challenge of working on what they were constitutionally born with – the shape of their face, the texture of their skin and hair, the size of their lips, and so on. In addition women share the common matters of sweating from certain parts of their bodies and, for a number of days each month, having blood streaming from them. Some consider themselves further burdened by having hair sprouting from parts of their bodies where, depending on fashion and social mores of the time, it is not considered aesthetic for it to do so. Perspiration, mensuration and hairiness are all areas needing attention, yet have, in history, largely been matters not spoken of openly let alone featured in the advertising columns of newspapers and magazines.

Concerns with perspiration, its smell and its affect on clothing, were largely dealt with by masking the odour with perfume and preventing staining by attaching protection pads to clothing. Actually human perspiration is relatively odourless but only comes to smell in hot and humid conditions when fermented by bacteria.

Bu-to, 'The odourless depilatory',
Home Notes, August 1939.

Commercial products dealing with perspiration did not come on to the market until the late nineteenth century – some as deodorants (targeting the bacteria), others as antiperspirants (targeting the actual sweat production). The first trade marked deodorant recorded was Mum, in 1888.

When it comes to publicity and advertising it was Odo-ro-no that really broke the taboo surrounding the subject . It was developed from an ophthalmic practice, that of Dr. Abraham D. Murphey of Cincinnati, who devised a liquid to reduce hand sweating in eye operating theatres. His daughter, Edna, tried it on herself, and, still a teenager, decided to run with it as a commercial possibility – a commercial deodorant.

Edna started writing the advertisements herself, but by 1914 was able to hire in J. Walter Thompson's agency. A Thompson upstart, James Young, decided to boost sales by promoting sweating as a social problem, exploiting feminine vulnerability in this matter. His first advertisement, in 1919, arrived with the heading – 'within the curve of a women's arm…':

> A woman's arm! Poets have sung of it, great artists have painted its beauty. It should be the daintiest, sweetest thing in the world. And yet, unfortunately, it isn't always.

This threatening line of copy continued to be taken by Odo-ro-no, a typical advertisement, in a 1933 *Home Notes*, used the tag 'Fatal to

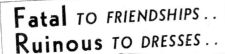

Fatal TO FRIENDSHIPS..
Ruinous TO DRESSES..

PERSPIRATION CAN COST YOU BOTH

Even if you *can* afford to ruin good dresses with unsightly perspiration stains, you surely shouldn't risk offending your friends with perspiration odour.

Odorono saves you from doing either. A doctor's prescription, it safely and efficiently controls perspiration and its odour.

Odorono is the famous, original perspiration preventive. Odorono Regular (ruby-red) gives the longest protection of any product of its kind. You use it just once or twice a week. The new type — quick-drying Instant Odorono (colourless) is formulated for women who prefer to use Odorono every day.

So Convenient

BOTH TYPES HAVE THE ORIGINAL ODO·RO·NO HYGIENIC APPLICATOR

Enclosed is 4d. in stamps for samples of Instant Odorono, Odorono Regular and Deodorant Crème Odorono.
NORTHAM WARREN, LTD. (Dept. S35), 215, Blackfriars Road, LONDON. S.E.1

Name ....

Address ....

ODO·RO·NO

Be twice as sweet

AS YOU ARE

WITH NEW

ODO·RO·NO -
Spray DEODORANT

BECAUSE IT'S

Twice as good

At your store or chemists now

Now, for the first time, the sensational new Odorono Spray—just two seconds to stop perspiration and give full 24-hour protection. Convenient to use—just spray it on and wipe off the excess. Economical, too—leak-proof, flexible bottle gives hundreds of sprays.

D.S.

Odo-ro-no, 'So Convenient', *Home Notes*, September 1933.

Odo-ro-no, 'Be twice as sweet', *Milady*, June 1952.

'Mum is the word!', press advert
and poster design, *c.* 1923.

'Now there is … Mum Lotion',
Picture Post, July 1939.

Picture Post, July 1, 1939

I NEVER HAVE A GOOD TIME AT THESE DARN DANCES

YOU SOUND LIKE JANE – BEFORE SHE USED **MUM** !

DON'T risk that greatest of social offences, perspiration odour. Use MUM. No matter how warm the weather, how strenuous the exercise, MUM, the cream deodorant, kills perspiration odour in an instant and yet does NOT stop perspiration. 30 seconds with MUM and you're safe for the day. Safe and easy to use, harmless to skin and clothing. Be safe. Be sure. Buy MUM.

SAMPLE—3d. in stamps will bring you generous sample. Write your name and address in BLOCK CAPITALS. Send to "MUM," Fassett and Johnson, Ltd. (Box P.P.3), 86 Clerkenwell Road, London, E.C.1.

MUM At all good Stores and Chemists **6d.,** 1/6 and 2/6

TAKES THE ODOUR OUT OF PERSPIRATION

Friendship'; another, another in 1942, picturing a tube train carried the copy 'In crowded places, think of your neighbour'. This line was also taken by Odo-ro-no's competitor Mum as, in a *Picture Post* of 1939, one friend confides to another: 'I never have a good time at these dances', with her friend replying: 'You sound like Jane before she used Mum'.

Along with the 'social outcast' line, each deodorant advertiser tried to distinguish its product by claims as to its' speed of working, period over which its effect lasted, its harmlessness to the skin, and how it protected clothes. Most all such products ensured at least 'day-long' freshness, Odo-ro-no claiming that although it could be used daily, it normally only needed to be used 'once or twice a week'. Mum declared it only needed 30 seconds to apply, Sno-mist only 10, and GO only 4! Odo-ro-no battled sweat 'ruinous to dresses', and avowed that by using it 'your clothes would be protected and your charm'; whilst Go claimed it 'never stained', and so on. Very few explained how their preparation actually worked, or tried to win customers over with scientific jargon, although there were occasional stabs at this, as in the 1950s Revlon would refer to its use of 'Lanolite', whilst Go killed the cause of odour with 'hexachlorophene'.

Deodorants and anti-perspirants were to come in a variety of forms – liquids, creams, powder, roll-ons, aero-sprays. Some names were obvious as Odo-ro-no (Odour Oh No!); others hinted at secrecy and social ostracism as 'Mum', 'Gossip' and 'Ban'. In the 1940s and 50s men became the market target, and then, into the 60s, the later

Go stick deodorant,
Picture Post, June 1956.

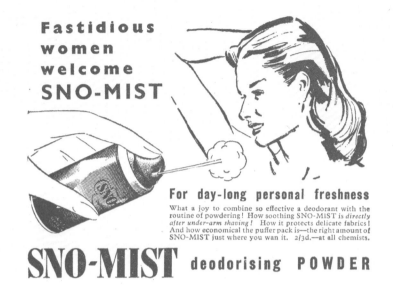

competitors 'fresh n'dainty' and FDS (Feminine Deodorant Spray) both began to stress the need for daily use not just with a 'period' as with the 'fresh n'dainty' advertisement:

> NOW! Be sure of your personal freshness every day of the month.

Whilst FDS similarly advised its users:

> 31 days a month – here is all the serenity, confidence, peace of mind you need.

No Offence!
it's friendly GOSSIP

The fresh, fragrant deodorant which charms away any suspicion of unpleasantness. Today, ask your chemist for GOSSIP Deodorant . . . in the plastic spray container, or attractive bottles, which can be used as refills.

GOSSIP DEODORANT CONTAINS WONDERFUL G. II

by dermacutt

Serenity and confidence. Find them, in FDS. FDS. The vaginal deodorant spray that's gentle, lightly scented . . . almost intimate. Here is all the serenity, confidence, peace of mind you need. Fragrant FDS, feminine deodorant spray. For thirty-one days of the month.

Opposite page, main image: Sno-mist deodorising powder, *Lilliput*, July 1949.

Above right: Gossip by Dermacutt, *Milady*, August 1957.

Above far right: FDS advert, *Vogue*, June 1969.

That the word 'vaginal' began to creep into advertisements shows how far social mores had moved from the young Edna Murphy trying to push her under-arm lotion at the beginning of the twentieth century.

It must have been galling for those women obsessed with being attractive to realize that for much of their lives, for some five or six days a month, they could be judged 'unclean', certainly 'untouchable', and, in certain eras, even considered 'evil'. The history and anthropology of the 'period' is patchy but certainly some measure of isolation would not have been uncommon.

Woman had to handle the 'curse', as it came to be known, as well as they could. In Western society, at best, with re-washable

NOW!
Be sure
of your
personal
freshness
every day
of the
month!

**Feminine deodorant ensures
intimate hygiene—all year round**

● Fresh 'n Dainty is new and different —
specifically formulated to deodorise
natural body secretions of the outer vaginal area.

● Delicately perfumed and medicated with a
soothing antiseptic for the most delicate tissues.

● Particularly useful during menstruation,
when travelling, and after physical exercise.

● Immediately refreshing and effective
for your everyday confidence.

**Get Fresh 'n Dainty today from your
chemist or department store**

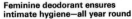

fresh'n dainty

deodorant dry spray
(70 gm) 8/8d
deodorant tissues
(6 sachets) 2/10d
'24 sachets' 7/11d
deodorant powder
(82 gm) 5/4d

Manufactured under licence by
Gerhardt-Penick Ltd
London Paris New York

Fresh'n dainty, c. 1968.

remnants of cloth, oftimes they might go without any protection. It was not until the late nineteenth century that commercially available disposable products came on to the market, the earliest said to be in Germany, in England Southall's, Rendell's, Mene, and Lilia, and in America Kimberly-Clarks Kotex and Johnson & Johnson's 'Modess'.

Because of the embarrassment surrounding their product early manufacturers actually found some difficulty in getting distributors, and although they mostly sold through chemists shops some found drapers and outfitters potential outlets, marketing their goods as part of women's underwear, particularly useful for 'ladies travelling by land and sea' as a Southall's advertisements proclaimed. A partner in the Southall's company wrote of 'the squeamishness of the draper to stock the goods seemed to be obstinately insuperable'.

For both distribution and advertising discretion was considered paramount. When samples were sent by post the buyer was assured they would be 'sent in a plain wrapper', and that all requests would be handled only by female staff. Shops had their assistants take off the recognizable outer cover before handing a purchase over to a customer; some even had facilities where the would-be purchaser put the money in a box and took the required packet without having to speak of the matter to a shop assistant.

When it came to advertising towels, many of the early examples included images of nurses and recommendations by doctors, stressing the hygiene advantages of disposable towels or pads – as Hartman's had it – 'a true health safeguard'. Much of such pussy-footing was to

Free from Care

To be free from all worry and enjoy hygienic safety to the utmost degree—use Mene, the modern hygiene. At work or play, you'll find Mene a real boon—not merely for their wonderful comfort, but for the perfect protection they give you all day long. Be sure to ask for Mene by name—they cost no more.

Prices 1'- & 1/2 in doz. pkts.   Larger Sizes 1/6, 2'- & 2/3.
Also in 6d. pkts. in the 1/-, 1/2 and 1/6 sizes

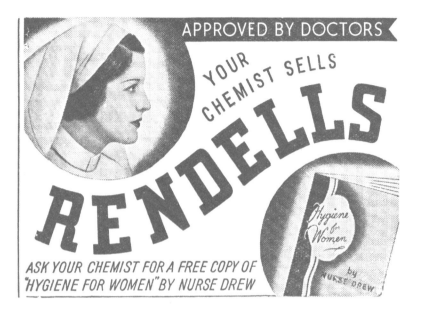

Above: Mene, 'Free from Care', *Home Notes*, September 1933.

Above right: Rendells advert, *Woman's Journal*, May 1937.

disappear by the 1920s. Although such factors as absorbency, non-chaffing and disposability continued to be included in advertising copy these matters came to be viewed as obvious essentials. Advertising began to take a different line – here was an item that gave women freedom, they could dance and dine and be fascinating every day of the month, without fear of detection, especially key then with the radical change in women's fashions.

The advertising of the 1920s and 30s no longer contained complex technical drawings of support belts and such. The inter-war years portray the emancipated woman – on the ski-slopes,

LET LILIA safeguard your health
and personal daintiness . . . .
LET LILIA give you uninterrupt-
ed comfort and a new freedom—in
your games and in your work . . .
LET LILIA save you inconveni-
ence and embarrassments . . . .
If you don't already know Lilia, you *must* try them now,
Send for samples and the invaluable handbook, "Plain
Words to Women" (written by a lady doctor), which sets a new
standard of freedom and well-being for all women all the time

LILIA
THE BRITISH SOLUBLE SANITARY TOWEL
Standard size, 1/- per carton of 12, with loops (or without
them)
SPECIAL OFFER TO NEW USERS.
*Twelve assorted Lilia towels, together with a new adjustable,
narrow, elastic suspender belt which has been medically approved, and one pair modern style protective knickers, for 3/6,
postfree. Towels and suspender, 2/-. Towels alone 1/3. Medical
handbook by a lady doctor in every package. Write : Miss D.
Downing (Dept. G113), Sashena Ltd., Lilia Works, Bartholo-
mew Road, London, N.W.5.
Awarded the Certificate of the Institute of Hygiene*

Above: Lilia, 'The British Soluble Sanitary Towel', *Home Notes*, September 1933.

Opposite page, left: Southalls, 'The name you can trust', *Woman's Magazine*, March 1934.

hiking in the countryside, in tennis gear and driving sports cars. A Modess advertisement in *Home Notes* in 1939 was typical, with its '5 more days to Live'. And British manufacturers, in the face of American competition, would emphasise their origins, their long years of serving the community, and appeal to women's patriotism. Lilia declared itself as the seller of 'The British Soluble Towel', whilst Southall's, was, in 1934, able to claim it had been in the towel market for over fifty years.

And then came Tampax! Tampax had been patented as early as 1931 by a Denver doctor who had been appalled by the 'rags' his wife was using. There had been earlier attempts to produce an internal pad but Earle Haas was the first to offer it with an applicator. Turned down by the giant Johnson & Johnson (who must have bitterly regretted its decision in hindsight), the patent was bought by a German immigrant, Gertrude Tenderich, and it was she who brought Tampax to the market in 1937, with the help of the advertising agency McCann Erikson. Although minnows soon arrived as competitors, it was Tampax who was to be the leader.

Although it continued to use medical support in its advertising, stressing its invention by a doctor and its wholesale use by nurses, Tampax took the 'freedom' line even further with 'no belts, no pins, no pads', along with such tags as 'Tampax is freedom exemplified'. And then it added a beauty dimension., as in a 1949 'Homes & Gardens advertisement:

Right: Wondersoft Kotex, *Woman's Journal*, May 1935.

Far right: Kotex Sanitary Towels, undated.

No other name enjoys so completely the trust and confidence of women in all walks of life as that of "Southalls"—makers of Sanitary Towels for over 50 years.

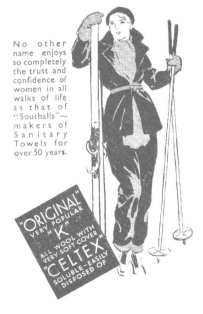

"I actually got into the semi-final and I should have been playing a girl I've often beaten. And then I had to stand down!"

" Why, whatever for ? Surely you know by now there's no need to do that nowadays. . . . Yes, perfect comfort — it's WONDERSOFT KOTEX. Listen . . "

Never Anxious
NOW!

WONDERSOFT Kotex is ideal for the outdoor girl. The sides are covered with downy-soft cotton-wool so that it cannot chafe the tenderest skin. Then WONDERSOFT Kotex never twists out of shape or 'pulls'—it keeps re-adjusting itself to conform to the body, no matter how active you are. The smooth, flat ends are *invisible* under the closest-fitting sports frock.

9d. for 6 pads — 1/6 for 12 (except in I.F.S.)

WONDERSOFT KOTEX
SANITARY PADS

Must every month bring

UNEASE AND DISCOMFORT?

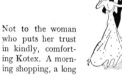

Not to the woman who puts her trust in kindly, comforting Kotex. A morning shopping, a long walk, an evening dancing—and Kotex remains as comfortable as ever.

So many intimate points of comfort belong to Kotex alone. Its sides are cushioned to make rubbing and chafing impossible. Kotex never fails—its hygienic padding is five times as absorbent as cotton wool. It stays soft—a miracle equaliser keeps moisture evenly spread. It never twists out of shape being modelled to your body, never shows because the tips are tapered. Find out from Kotex what unfailing comfort means.

With or without loops

6d. FOR 6 PADS
1/- FOR 12 PADS

BLUE BOX—fitted with loops   GREEN BOX—without loops
BROWN BOX—super—for extra protection. 1/6d. for 12 pads

KOTEX *are comforting*
SANITARY TOWELS

CAN'T CHAFE - CAN'T FAIL - CAN'T SHOW
Prices do not apply in Eire

Modess, '5 Days More to Live',
Home Notes, August 1939.

Tampax, *Home Notes*, June 1940.

Tampax, *Housewife*, July 1945.

Modern women
especially appreciate
the easy and hygienic
insertion assured by
the Tampax
individual applicator

NO BELTS
NO PINS
NO PADS

Packets of ten, 1/9

Tampax Ltd., Belvue Road, Northolt, Middlesex

PRIDE
—AND POISE

With every eye upon her, she smiles in her hour of
triumph, radiant and proud. Happy the women, who
enjoy the social and sporting round, poised and
supremely self-confident, no matter what the calendar
date. Tampax, the completely modern, completely
different sanitary protection, ensures daintiness and
good grooming, gives that all-important sense of
security even when the flimsiest finery *is de rigueur*.

Because Tampax is *worn internally*, you can wear it
and forget it. Chafing or other embarrassments are impossible with Tampax. No one knows your secret but
yourself. It is neater, more discreet, more hygienic and
infinitely more comfortable than outmoded methods.

THANKS TO
TAMPAX
Sanitary Protection Worn Internally

TAMPAX LIMITED, BELVUE ROAD, NORTHOLT, MIDDLESEX.

Good Housekeeping, 1952.

Freedom to enjoy every moment of your holiday, to bake and
bathe and laze and look your loveliest no matter what the date.

In a 1952 advertisement in 'Good Housekeeping' Tampax focuses
entirely on its contribution to a woman's ability to fascinate,
describing a woman at the races:

> With every eye upon her, she smiles in her hour of triumph,
> radiant and proud. Happy the women who enjoy the social and
> sporting round poised and supremely confident no matter what
> the calendar date…no one knows your secret but yourself.

Although the somewhat limited literature on the advertising of
sanitary towels suggests that in their early years only the classier
magazines were used because the product was expensive, many
examples can be found in the more homely publications as *Home
Notes* and *Home Chat*. And, indeed, for the inter-war years an
argument can be made that such advertising occurred more in the
workaday press than in the *Vogue* and *Country Life*!

Nevertheless a brief surveying of the advertising scene does
suggest that whatever the level of the journal, a classiness imbued
the images and the copy, with much reference to holidays and sport,
of formal dances and social events, and not a sight of a working
woman whether lawyer or waitress. Even when Southall's mentions
'well-educated women' purchasers, the illustration is of an exquisitely

Home, May 1961.

manicured hand showing not a trace of manual labour. But did the average working woman continue to use 'rags' and have suspicion of the potential danger of an internal tampon? Statistics are scarce but would almost certainly show a cascading down from the fashionable leisure-loving upper classes.

As mentioned in the section on hair, this was only considered an asset when it was judged, by any culture, to be on the appropriate part of the body. Back to Neolithic times customs have decreed what was desirable and what not when it came to body hair. With women, hair was generally admired on the head, eyebrows and eyelashes, but elsewhere, when it came to Western culture, hair has been considered unaesthetic, unattractive, unhygienic and embarrassing.

A very basic method for getting rid of unwanted hair has been literally to tear it out, whether as with early cultures such articles as sea shells, or, in the twentieth century, tweezers, razors, wax and eventually electrolysis and lasers; the aim has been to remove hair, and, if possible, prevent it reappearing. Chemical depilatories came to be developed in a variety of forms – gels, creams, lotions, roll-ons, aerosols and powder.

Getting rid of particular patches of hair became a fashion imperative after WWI with short and sleeveless dresses and increasingly scanty beachwear. An advertisement for BU-TO, an odourless depilatory of the inter-war years, had as its copy, beneath an image of a grandma with a teen-age granddaughter:

92

SECRET AGENT!

The Queen, June 1961.

You certainly show a lot of yourself, Lucy – but I can't say I object, your skin is so smooth and pretty! But then there's really no excuse at all for unsightly hair – now that you lucky girls have BU-TO to whisk it away.

Although a number of depilatories were developed before WWI, the dominating brand after the war was VEET, first registered in 1919, produced by the Hannibal Pharmaceutical Company of Canada (variably marketed in different parts of the world at different times as NEET and Immac).

VEET, hyped as 'an amazing discovery of SCIENCE', by reducing the strength of keratin in hair, meant that, after a short time, surplus hair could just be wiped away. The tag declared 'in just 3 minutes'. Competing with the razor, it claimed to leave the skin smooth, no stubbly, to avoid coarse regrowth, and to be painless. To compete with other creams VEET would stress that it was 'sweet smelling'.

Gilette had actually marketed a razor for women in the 1910s – the Milady Décolleté; Remington did not produce one until the 1940s. But parallel to the development of creams and razors were experiments with electrolysis, aiming to remove unwanted hair permanently. Early tests were actually for a different purpose, for removing ingrowing eyelashes, a problem often presented to ophthalmologists. Work in America and France resulted in a technology that could be used by lay electrologists by which electricity was applied directly to the hair follicle.

VEET
A CREAM THAT REMOVES HAIR.

How to have Smooth White Arms
Absolutely Free of All Hair Growth

Nothing is so repellent and disillusioning as hair growth on the arms of a woman. Every suggestion of daintiness is instantly destroyed. For removing objectionable hair growths of any kind there is nothing so effective and pleasant to use as Veet. Veet is a new perfumed velvety cream that has entirely superseded noxious, dangerous depilatories. It **is** far better than scraping razors which only make the hair grow faster and thicker each time they are used. Whereas ordinary depilatories and razors merely remove hair *above* the skin surface, Veet melts the hair away *beneath* it. It is as easy to use as a face cream. Simply spread it on as it comes from the tube, wait a few minutes, rinse it off and the hair is gone as if by magic. The many and obvious uses of Veet will appeal to all women. Satisfactory results guaranteed in every case or money is returned. Veet may be obtained for 3/6 at all chemists, hairdressers and stores, or it is sent post paid in plain wrapper for 4/-. (Trial size by post for 6d. in stamps.) Dae Health Laboratories (Dept. 267M),68,Bolsover Street, London, W.1.

WHY I USE NEW VEET

1. *New 'Veet'* ends all unwanted hair in 3 minutes without trouble, mess or bother.
2. *New 'Veet'* leaves the skin soft, smooth and white without trace of ugly stubble.
3. *New 'Veet'* is a dainty white cream — sweetly scented and pleasant to use.
4. *New 'Veet'* avoids coarse re-growth—unlike the razor which only makes the hair grow faster and thicker. 1/3 and 2/6 (Trial size 6d.).

Although a *Picture Post* advertisement in 1939 showed a 'home-kit' 'so simple a child could use it', as supplied to 'Royal Houses of Europe and Asia', more usually an aura of mystery and pseudo-medicalism surrounded electrolysis, no more so than at the Tao Clinics, which spread rapidly through Britain in the post-WWII years. Started by a Mrs. Eileen Ingram, who, with a fascination for all things oriental thought up the name Tao (in Mandarin 'the right path') set up her first clinic in London. Unlike other methods of hair removal for which advertising was largely in the popular press, Mrs. Ingram's publicity was to be found in *Vogue* or *The Queen*, and often included the nugget that her clinic was only 'seven doors down from Harrods'. Although some date the first Tao clinic as 1948, a 1960 advertisement noted '20 years experience', and a 1967 one raised this to 30, suggesting that Mrs. Ingram was already active in the 1930s. By the 1960s there were over twenty branches, Harrods setting up its own electrolysis department!

By the 1960s removing unwanted hair for beautification had become common practice, and methods widely advertised, only differing in their claims as to speed, painlessness and permanency – sweat smells, hairiness and periods had been openly accepted as human, as natural, but for attractiveness, as needing control.

BRYLCREEM

IN THE HANDY ACTIVE SERVICE TUBE

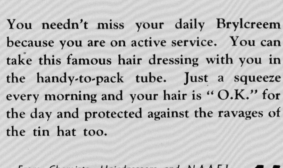

You needn't miss your daily Brylcreem because you are on active service. You can take this famous hair dressing with you in the handy-to-pack tube. Just a squeeze every morning and your hair is "O.K." for the day and protected against the ravages of the tin hat too.

From Chemists, Hairdressers and N.A.A.F.I. everywhere in tubes, bottles or jars

1/-

Larger bottles 1/6, 1/9, 2/6

BRYLCREEM THE PERFECT HAIR DRESSING

County Perfumery Co., Ltd., North Circular Road, West Twyford, London, N.W.10

Royd

For Men

One current advertisement for men's 'beauty' products includes Age-Rebel Moisturiser, Postshave Rescue, Age-Rebel Eye Hydrator and Triple Action Grooming Oil; L'Oréal are offering Paris Men Expert Barber Club Pomade, Expert Hydra Energetic Cooling Eye Roll-On, Paris Men Expert Carbon Protest Deodorant, along with beard oil, wrinkle eye cream and charcoal face mask; whilst MMUK have foundations, concealers, cream finishers, bronzing powder, brow gel, beard filler, eyeliner, lengthening mascara, and brushes to go with it.

Although the actual words may be unknown to a beau, dandy, or 'macaroni' of the eighteenth century, the functions of such products would be familiar. From ancient Egypt and before, through to the nineteenth century, men applied themselves with preparations. Such activity might have been to placate the gods or as a protection from the elements. A good deal of it was to show off status, to hold on to the beauty of youth, and, indeed, to attract, as in the courts of Elizabeth and James, the firsts, where rosemary

Opposite page: Brylcreem advert, *Picture Post*, December 1939.

97

water would be applied to the hair, honey and egg masks used for the wrinkles, and powders used to lighten the skin, amongst an array of other wares.

It is only in the Victorian era that spending time on male grooming came to be considered unnecessary, indeed unmanly. What little grooming was required would be done by one's valet or at the barber's shop. Men needed to appear washed and well-trimmed, but that was sufficient. What few products that were on the market largely related to head hair – hair, moustache and beard – as Rowland's Macassar Oil, Atkinson's curling fluid and Edward Pinaud's brilliantine. Price & Gosnell, from the mid-nineteenth century, were producing, along with their perfumes and soaps, such products as bear's grease for hair loss, and pomade Hongroise for moustaches. Yardley's, similarly largely known for its perfumes and soaps, was, at the turn of the century, selling brilliantines and shaving sticks.

In the period covered here, men's grooming again largely related to hair – hair on the top of the head to be kept neat, or, if thinning, to be replaced, and hair around the mouth – moustache and beard – that needed shaving and shaping. It was in 1928 that what was to become a market leader was launched in Birmingham by the County Chemical Company, a firm at the time producing lubricants, household cleaning products, adhesives and such like. Brylcreem was initially only marketed through barber shops, but when it came to be advertised to the masses the message accompanying it was that it would make hair both healthy and lustrous (without excessive

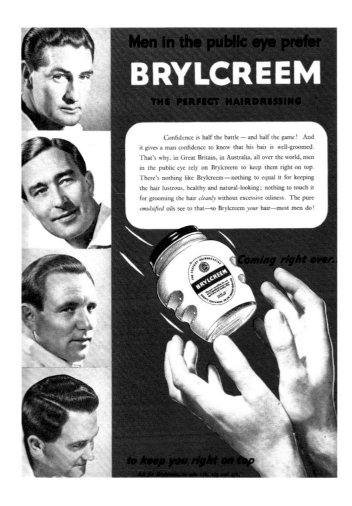

Here's a man looking his smartest—and a girl who knows it! But good grooming isn't a thing for special occasions only. It matters *every* day. Dry, brittle, scruffy hair—hair that's full of dandruff—it hardly makes an attractive picture. That's why you should always use Silvikrin Hair Dressing or Hair Cream.

Enriched with Pure Silvikrin, the hair's natural food, these famous Silvikrin products feed health into your hair. And healthy hair is the basis of good grooming.

FOR WELL-GROOMED, HEALTHY HAIR, USE

Silvikrin

HAIR DRESSING OR **HAIR CREAM**

(A Lotion with Oil) 2/6d. and 4/4½d. a bottle   2/9d. a jar

'Men in the public eye prefer Brylcreem',
John Bull, August 1953.

'For well-groomed, healthy hair, use
Silvikrin', *Men Only*, September 1955.

How's that for a fine head of Hair!

Use Pure Silvikrin in severe cases of dandruff and thinning hair. As a daily dressing use Silvikrin Hair Tonic Lotion or, for dry heads, the new Silvikrin Hair Tonic Lotion with Oil.

21/E/U

Silvikrin
THE HAIR'S NATURAL FOOD

oil) – 'no gum, no soap, no spirit, no starch' – 'it grooms without gumming'. What was promised was that by using it one would gain confidence and thereby succeed – 'the perfect hair-dressing to keep you well on top' was punned.

The macho image conveyed by Brylcreem advertisements was touched by glamour when, during WWII, members of the Royal Air Force came to be known as the Brylcreem boys. If well-known personalities were used in its advertisements they would tend to be sportsmen rather than people in show business (it was Beckham who became the face of Brylcreem in the 1990s). The appearance of women in the advertisements was a rarity.

The reverse was true for Brylcreem's competitor, Silvikrin, marketed by the German company Wella. Franz Stroher invented a waterproof product that would 'allow the scalp to breathe', and from such beginnings grew an international company selling not only hair products but equipment for hair perming and dyeing. Silvikrin was advertised as unisex, with separate advertising for the male and female markets, but for advertising to men there was often a woman or two portrayed as well. One such had two women gossiping with a man nearby – 'How's that for a fine head of hair'; another had a couple at the altar, she glancing shyly sideways with the copy 'Here's a man looking his smartest – and a girl who knows it'.

A third product in the genre, never, perhaps, with quite the glamour of Brylcreem and Silvikrin was Cheseborough's Vaseline Hair Tonic. This was not only advertised to keep hair 'manageable

Opposite page: Silvikrin, 'How's that for a fine head of Hair!', *The Strand*, May 1949.

and handsome' but to stimulate the circulation of the oils in the scalp
and tackle dryness in the texture of the hair. Vaseline Hair Tonic
advertisements frequently included the odd woman, invariably eyeing
'a man who means to go places', and clearly seeing him as attractive
– 'you're only as handsome as your hair' – linking hair preparations
with good-looks. As with Vaseline Hair Tonic, Evan Williams
shampoo, marketed from the 1920s, although more often indicated as
for women, was sometimes focused on men as well, later to stress its
men's appeal by being packed in a stainless steel container resembling
a hip flask.

It appears that men's hair products have as much, if not
more, been advertised to stir men's ambitions – to be smart, to be
successful, to get ahead – as much as to be more sexually attractive,
more handsome. Nevertheless there is an indication throughout the
advertising (until the 60s and 70s when men's hair began to flow more
freely) that the woman in the street preferred men with smooth, glossy
(but not greasy) well-groomed hair.

When it comes to men grooming hair on the lower part of their
faces – moustaches and beards – over the centuries fashion has swung
this way and that. Historians record high status Egyptians actually
sporting false metal beards, Romans having their beards cut by their
slaves, the court of Charles I liking beards trimmed and so on. But for
the period of this book, 1920–1970, faces were largely free of beards
with the occasional appearance of the moustache, modeled on such
film stars as Ronald Colman and Clark Gable; and, during the war and

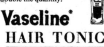

Wilkinson, 'The Safety Razor with Hollow Ground Blades', 1923.

beyond, what was known as the RAF handlebar, the radio comedian Jimmy Edwards forming the Handle Bar Club.

The essential grooming product for all this coming and going was the razor. Early evidence suggests that anything lying at hand might have been used for cutting, as shells or flints, but eventually a metal blade emerged as standard, coming, in Victorian times, to be referred to as a 'cut-throat' for the very reason that although it functioned reasonably well to remove hair from the chin and around the mouth, if carelessly used would result in nicks and scratches of the skin. Men of wealth would have had their valets wield the razor, but with the growth of barber shops, it became customary to have the barber shave, or at least trim, to the fashion of the time.

Safety razors did not come on to the market until the turn of the century. The first, developed in the United States, sported blades that needed stropping and honing, just like the 'cut-throat'. In England, Wilkinson's Sword Company introduced a 'safety' razor that had a holder with a detachable blade, but, again, the blade needed sharpening; later the blades were modified to be disposable. The company's advertising, through to WWII, emphasized the considerable reputation it had built as a producer of cutting instruments, as one in 1939:

> The same steel that made Wilkinson's Sword famous ever since Inkerman, is the steel that is in the Wilkinson Hollow-ground blade.

Above: Gillette, 'All set for luxury shaves', *Punch*, October 1935.

Above right: Series of adverts for Gillette, by Crawford's advertising agency, 1939.

But it was King Camp Gillette of Boston who developed what was to become the most popular razor with disposable blades, which was to be distributed to the entire American armed services in WWI. Advertising for the Gillette Safety Razor tended to emphasise its advanced technical production – 'years of research', 'electrically tempered', 'precision made' – and also gave it a kind of kudos of tradition (albeit a short one) of being made by skilled craftsmen, even that it was English (which originally it was not).

Men who bought a Gillette razor were not necessarily promised to be made more handsome, but to be endowed with more wisdom and commonsense and, as a result to gain respect. Occasionally the odd advertisement did suggest some admiration from women might result, as one that had a woman stroking a man's cheek – 'You'll be glad you gave him a Gillette'. The Gillette came to be hyped as what

a woman might give a man as a present – a typical advertisement having a little boy telling his mother 'I know what daddy would like for Christmas'.

One of the most notable campaigns for Gillette was devised by Crawford's advertising agency in 1939. This consisted of a series of 'uniformed' workers, from judges and service men to bus drivers, with relevant copy as to how essential their Gillette was to them. Later Crawford, with coloured advertisements, was to introduce what was to become a common catchphrase – 'Good Mornings begin with Gillette'.

But it was the Gillette advertisements using the graphic designer Tom Eckersley, that perhaps most caught the eye of the public, and that made buyers of Gillette appreciate they were part of a universal horde. With copy headings as 'they have made the world clean-shaven', and 'all over the world', Gillette swaggered its top position in the shaving market. Eckersley, who had been an ailing child filling his time with drawing, had, by the onset of WWII built up a considerable reputation for himself, in partnership with a fellow art school student, Eric Lombers. After a period in the RAF as a cartographer, Eckersley was to combine commissioned work with teaching at the London College of Printing. His Gillette advertisement became iconic, featuring two heads facing each other, one bearded and one clean-shaven – heads of people of different nationalities as well as heads of animals as lions and goats.

Gillettes' main competitor was EverReady, the company having been launched in 1905 by German brothers, Frederick, Otto and

Opposite page: 'Good mornings begin with Gillette', one of a series by Tom Eckersley, *c.* 1948.

Richard Kempfe. They had set up a tool shop in New York and from that came the idea of producing safety razors. Ever Ready's advertising in England, particularly after WWII, was altogether more directly targeted at women as potential purchasers. A razor was something women bought for their menfolk for which due appreciation would be shown. Advertising copy sported such headings as 'he will remember you with gratitude every morning when he uses his magnificent Streamline Ever Ready Razor Set', and '5 million women can't be wrong'; women being particularly targeted in the run up to Christmas. One advertisement has a woman, with pencil poised, making her present list – 'If it's a man it's an Ever Ready'; a similar one has a woman peeping round the bathroom door as her man is shaving – 'The perfect Christmas gift'. Along with this particular line it was Ever Ready, which introduced the '5 o'clock shadow', emphasizing that its razor provided such a close shave that it would last 'all day and all evening'.

Then came the electric razor with Philips dominating the British market with Philishave, its advertising blinding by science – '36,000 shaving actions a minute'. The electric razor became the norm in that it both avoided nicks and tearing, offered a really close shave (by stretching the skin), and, above everything, was economical, for although expensive to buy it saved time in daily use and did not need constant blade buying. In hindsight it seems quite quaint that British razor advertising, certainly in the fifties, used radio personalities of the time, particularly comedians, as Philishave with Jack Train and Ever

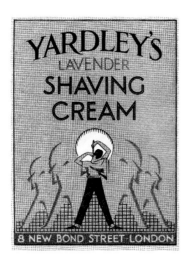

"Ah! that reminds me to **Get Gibbs!**"

It's Super-Fatted!

This means that Gibbs Super-Fatted Shaving Cream gives a richer, more creamy lather—a lather that stays moist—your razor will cut close—no need to go over the tough places twice. Super-fatting also ensures an after-feeling of delightful ease and refreshment because it gives something back to the skin. CHANGE TO GIBBS TO-DAY!

GIBBS SUPER-FATTED **SHAVING CREAM**

D. & W. GIBBS LTD., LONDON, E.1.

Ready with Tommy Handley (tweaking his catch phrase 'it's that man again' into 'it's that beard again').

Along with razors the market was flooded with products to prepare the hair for being shaved, shaving soaps and creams, and after-shave products to round off the job. Beauty product historians would have it that some 3,000 years ago Sumerians used found materials to soften their hair. Fast forward to Georgian times when barbers of Old Bond Street, Truefit and Hill, were selling soaps, along with hair creams and tonics and scents. And then came Pear's, who by the early 1920's targeted men with its Opaque and its Ivostrip shaving stick, to be followed by Yardley's in the 1930s offering a lavender shaving cream and Gibbs, the toothpaste manufacturer, a 'super-fatted' cream.

Bradshaw, in his remarkable book on art in advertising, published in the early 1920's, wrote on advertising the shaving stick: 'The subject is a difficult one to express artistically'. What the advertiser had to express, either visually or in copy, was the comparative virtues of its products over all others – for producing lots of lather quickly, for smelling pleasant, the stick itself being firm, easily held, and it lasting a long time – no easy task.

One of the most popular British brands was Erasmic, which, like Pears, was selling its products to women as well. The company, founded in 1886, by the end of WWI, was so prosperous as to afford to take full pages for colour advertisements in magazines such as *Punch*. A remarkable Erasmic advertisement in 1923, actually shows a woman at the wheel of a sports car with a man carrying golf clubs standing

Opposite page, top: Showcard for Yardley's Lavender Cream, 1932.

Opposite page, bottom: Gibbs Super-Fatted Shaving Cream, *Illustrated London News*, May 1937.

Right: Erasmic Shaving Stick, *Punch*, October 1923.

Far right: Erasmic Shaving Creams, *Men Only*, November 1955.

alongside. The copy was full of puns, as: 'which is the shaving soap that doesn't encourage you to slice your drive with a razor?' The popularity of the product was suggested by the reader being invited to: 'step in with the millions of men who would no more dream of using other soaps, than they would play golf with a cricket bat'. Through to the 1950s Erasmic kept on with its upbeat style, by then preferring photography for its advertisements.

In the post-WWII years the advertisements for Shavello shaving cream, produced by Hudson & Knight, began to rival those of Erasmic with their more sparse copy and large font – 'Hello Shavello'. It too would resort to golfing puns such as 'You'll

You'll be round in fewer strokes with Shavallo. The rich creamy lather helps the razor to slip smoothly through the 'rough.'

SHAVALLO *Shaving Cream*

Selling Agents: HUDSON & KNIGHT, LTD.

S.V.179-51

Shavallo Shaving Cream, 'Hallo! Shavallo!', *Lilliput*, October 1949.

be around in a few strokes', and, 'help the razor to slip smoothly through the rough'; but more frequently women were sported eyeing men exclaiming 'Hello Shavello'.

After-shaves have been on the market prior to the arrival of the safety razor, as Rowland's Kalydor from the 1820's, and initially had been advertised to mop up after accidents with the cut-throat, as an antiseptic to prevent infection, and to reduce skin irritation; overtime they morphed into being sold as scents. One of the most popular brands – Old Spice – was in fact from an American company that had brought out scents for men and women in the late 1930s, before developing a full men's range to include shaving soap, after- shave and shampoo. Their advertising theme was naval, initially using ships as logos and, in the post-war years, actual photographs of seamen, along with such copy as 'Men who sail the seven seas choose the protection of Old Spice'. By this it hoped to put over a masculine aura to scented products that could otherwise have been seen as feminine.

Pre- and post-war shaving products came largely from soap or fragrance manufacturers expanding their product range, so that eventually everyone seemed to be offering everything needed, albeit sometimes the expanded range diluted the impact of the original product on which the company had been built. An example was Yardley's that had strayed into the men's market in the 1930s but eventually retreated into men's scents that they advertised as hair and body washes, its after-shave being marketed as 'after-shave-splash'.

It was the two feisty women, Helena Rubinstein and Elizabeth Arden, who dared to try their hands at marketing what might be described as products for improving men's attractiveness, beyond keeping them well trimmed. Rubinstein took as her second husband Prince Archil Gourelli Tchkonia, supposedly descended from Georgian royalty. This inspired her to launch the House of Gourelli range for men, its packaging bearing the Gourelli crest. Her salons suddenly sprouted 'grey' rooms, with separate entrances, offering herbal products for the skin, hair, teeth and body, along with boutiques of men's clothing. The concept never really caught the public's imagination and the House of Gorelli died with the prince's death in 1955.

Elizabeth Arden too took a prince as a second husband, in 1942, and demanded to be addressed thereby as princess. She

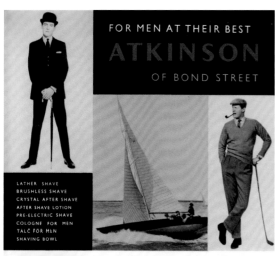

LATHER SHAVE
BRUSHLESS SHAVE
CRYSTAL AFTER SHAVE
AFTER SHAVE LOTION
PRE-ELECTRIC SHAVE
COLOGNE FOR MEN
TALC FOR MEN
SHAVING BOWL

There's something new on a man's curriculum. A collection of incredibly fine preparations for good grooming. Each one bears the world-famous name—Atkinson of Bond Street. From this great House comes, now, something rather special in manly comforts.

At last, a man can go into a shop, order shaving soap or lotion, talc or cologne, and know that he is doing the right thing. Moreover, a woman may buy these personal articles for the man in her life with confidence. Their excellence will be recognised by men the world over. And they meet needs that every civilised man has felt for years.

Shaving, for instance, now becomes both efficient and pleasurable. There is a

choice of three Atkinson essentials for the actual shaving itself: Brushless Cream, Lather Cream, and solid soap in a handsome wooden Shaving Bowl. For afterwards there are After Shave Lotion and Crystal After Shave (this last is a unique substance for the man who wants the freshness without the sting). For users of electric razors, there is a Pre-Electric Lotion. Two more products complete the range—Talc and Cologne.

All eight have about them a mild aromatic quality—very slightly sharp, very clearly masculine. These splendid preparations by Atkinson of Bond Street are in the shops now. Men will be glad to get them—women will be thanked for giving them. They cost 6/6 to 12/6.

Give him the big red one

You'll enjoy it as much as he does

Old Spice

1. Hair Cream, After Shave 15/9.   2. After Shave, Lather Shaving Cream 10/2.   3. Hair Cream 5/10.
4. Cologne, Hair Cream, Stick Deodorant, Shower Soap, After Shave, Body Talcum, After Shave Talcum 66/2.   5. Shaving Mug 12/8.
6. After Shave 6/8, 9/11, 17/9.   7. Aerosol Deodorant, After Shave Travel Pack, Hair Cream Tube 22/4.

SHULTON NEW YORK LONDON PARIS

Opposite page, left: Atkinson, 'For men at their best', *Country Life*, October 1960.

Opposite page, right: Old Spice, 'Give him the big red one', *Sunday Times Magazine*, 1966.

packaged her men's range in grey and gold, but instead of a crest had as logo a man on horseback, horses being her major passion. Along with after-shave balm and soap, she included lip balm and eau-de-cologne. Again the enterprise was doomed, this time on her divorce. It was not, perhaps, until the late 1950s that an authentic men's beauty product range was launched by Charles Revson – 'That Man' – named facetiously, as it was said that was how Rubinstein and Arden referred to him. None of these American essays in a man's range were advertised in Britain, Rubinstein suggesting that 'British Men were just not ready for skin care'.

Whereas women's beauty products were invariably linked to glamour and sexual attraction, men's toiletry advertising, for the period of the book, was more frequently linked to success, one of the most frequently employed word being 'smart', which has the dual meaning of attractive and clever. Where well-known personalities were used to hype the products they tended to be tough, masculine characters, most frequently sportsmen. If one used what was being advertised one would join other millions or so smart men who were going places, who were ambitious and achievers. Nevertheless, for a good deal of this advertising there was a hint that along with this would come a greater attraction to the female sex, at least enough to have them buy such for you as a present, if not make more blatant approaches.

Put your best face forward

Wartime

'For beauty on duty.'

Tangee lipstick advertisement, 1939

On the 3rd of September 1939 England declared war on Germany. In 1940 a series of Limitation of Supply Orders were introduced that controlled production across industries, reducing output to a fraction of what it had been in peacetime, even if an industry was allowed to continue producing its brands at all (for which it would get a quota allowance). Factory space had to be freed up for munitions; factory workers called up for the services, if what they were producing was considered inessential. Elizabeth Arden, with Teddy Haslam well-established in British society, received a high quota; Helena Rubinstein, with her representative Boris Foster a relative new-comer, a considerably lower one. Foster did what he could by trying to persuade other producers to sell him part of their quotas, but, in any case, with a tight budget for advertising, Rubinstein took something of a back seat in Britain during the war.

The Limitation of Supply Orders not only affected manufacturing space but rationed basic materials, as metal and petro-chemicals, so essential for the production and packaging of beauty

117

PUNCH ALMA?

Put your best face forward

To look lovely while you 'look lively' is a
big help to good morale, for good looks and a high
heart go together. Though "Yardleys" appear in
wartime packings nowadays, they still have all the
qualities you know and trust.

Yardley

BOND STREET COMPLEXION POWDER . BEAUTY CREAMS
HAND CREAM · TOILET SOAP *Lavender & Box Complexion* · LIPSTICK
ROUGE · TALCUM POWDER *Lavender and April Violets*.
Very may be difficult to obtain but they are worth searching for.

★ *If you have any war-time beauty problems write to Mary Foster,
the Yardley Beauty Consultant. She will be very glad to help.*

YARDLEY · 33 OLD BOND STREET · LONDON, W.1

products. A 1940 Tattoo advertisement advised 'metal makes guns,
keep your Tattoo holder'; other producers, as Gala, also took up the
idea of refills.

As women were less able to glamorize themselves with clothing
being rationed, they turned to make-up, which itself was in short
supply. Many resorted to home remedies, and very soon women's
magazines were featuring recipes for substitute creams and cosmetics
with such humble products as beetroot, boot polish, and flour and
paste. With silk imports curtailed, legs were stained with gravy, an
eyebrow pencil used to draw the seam of an unobtainable stocking.
Eventually the producers began to meet the need as Revlon with 'Leg
Silk' and Rubinstein's 'Velva Leg Film'.

Producers did what they could to optimize the situation both
in Britain and America, cozying up to serve wartime governments by
showing their patriotism, hoping to get increased quotas. All were at
it! In the States Revlon was making guns as well as first-aid kits for
the troops; Helena Rubinstein provided some 60,000 boxes for G.I.s
containing useful items as cleansers, sunburn cream, and camouflage
for troops on desert duty; Max Factor also had coloured make-up
for camouflage, as did Cyclax; Coty offered foot powder and anti-
gas ointment; Elizabeth Arden made contributions on both sides of
the Atlantic, with her make-up kit for the American Marine Corps
Women's Reserve (lipstick, rouge and nail varnish) and in England
worked with the British founder of plastic surgery, Sir Harold Delf
Gillies, to provide a tinted scar cream.

TANGEE
LIPSTICK
for Beauty on Duty

On duty she must look smart—but *not* painted. That's why TANGEE is the almost invariable choice of all women on National Service. TANGEE's miraculous colour-change gives lips the *exact* shade Natu e decrees will make them look their loveliest. Never be without TANGEE! It's the 'uniform' lipstick for **individual** loveliness.

Try TANGEE Theatrical for evening occasions when a brighter colour is required.

★ *Tangee special cream base prevents chapped lips.*

Tangee Lipstick for *YOUR individual colour,* **1/9** and **4/6**

Tangee Rouge to match. *Compact* **1/9** and **3/6.** *Crème* **3/6**

Tangee Face Powder *six shades* - **2/6** and **4/6**

6d. trial sizes obtainable everywhere

WHAT?
NO POWDER?

It's not the shopkeeper's fault !

Yardley are doing their utmost to keep your favourite Chemist or Store supplied, but Government restrictions, owing to war necessity, have severely limited stocks of Perfumes and Cosmetics ; **nevertheless there should be enough to go round if you will help by economising in their use.**

Most of the Yardley Perfumery and Beauty Products are going Overseas in support of our Nation's great Export Drive ; your sisters there have always loved them just as much as you do.

For generations, Yardley has been famed for the superlative quality of the delightful things which bear their name.

Use carefully those little refinements you still can enjoy — be scrupulous in your choice when you must replace, and remember — **Quality IS Economy.**

Yardley

33 OLD BOND STREET · LONDON

Above: Evan Williams Shampoo, *Picture Post*, November 1942.

Right: Tangee Lipstick, 'For Beauty on Duty', *Picture Post*, October 1939.

Far right: Yardley, 'What? No Powder?', *Illustrated London News*, May 1941.

CAUTIONARY TALE

Now that only a proportion of the pre-war supply of well-known cosmetics can be made, trusted preparations such as Pond's are difficult to get. So, if you have to buy creams bearing an unknown name or no name at all, be careful—for your complexion's sake. And, of course, when you are lucky enough to strike some Pond's, use it sparingly and do all you can to make it last as long as possible.

POND'S

Of course advertising itself was being seriously affected by shortage of paper and print with the German's invasion of Norway and the Russian's in Finland. Newsprint became rationed and launch of new publications was only allowed after special pleading. Advertising space was therefore limited, spaces became smaller and rates more expensive.

When it came to the content of advertising all manufacturers fairly quickly had any people appearing in their artwork now kitted out in service uniform – Brylcreem with its men in Royal Air Force garb, Odo-ro-no with its women in ATS, WAAF and WRNS outfits, and so on; Eugene Waves and Evan Williams shampoo decided on air raid wardens. The fact that nearly everyone was contributing to the war effort in one way or another did not mean that their appearances should be neglected and those not in the services were portrayed in the back gardens or allotments in suitable gear 'digging for victory' or in a factory appropriately aproned, but still using the advertised goods.

The actual messages in beauty preparations advertising were along the lines that people's sacrifices were helping the war effort and to keep up morale you ought to do what you can to make your appearance attractive. Advertisements began to carry copy explaining the situation and advising economy, as Nivea 'make Nivea last longer…use it sparingly'. Yardley was perhaps one of the most forthright and fulsome:

Yardley are doing their bit to keep your favourite chemist
or store supplied, but Government restrictions, owing to
war necessity, have severely limited stocks of perfumes and
cosmetics; nevertheless there should be enough to go round if
you will help by economizing their use.

Snowfire was more specific when it came to economy, as in an
advertisement in *Picture Post*: 'one good application a day', 'only use a
little', 'pat only certain spots', 'a dab will suffice'.

Producers of beauty products were determined to keep their
brand names in the public eye whether their goods were available or
not. Bulletins continued throughout the war reminding people of why
there were shortages, how they could economise, and what the future
held. Bourjois was one that was particularly active updating potential
customers as to the situation with 'do not pass a shop which sells
Bourjois products, the quota may just have arrived'. Coty continuously
carried patriotic but self-congratulatory copy reminding people that it
had 'spun a girdle of loveliness around the world':

Treasure your Coty to-day. The supply is strictly limited. The
beauty service that has made Coty famous must be a shadow
of its former self until Victory allows the development of our
comprehensive post-war plans.

By 1944 it had become increasingly optimistic:

Left: Snowfire, 'Make your make-up go further', *Picture Post*, August 1942.

Above: 'Make Nivea last longer', *Housewife*, February 1945.

123

Busy
War Workers
should remember

THE GREATER THE STRAIN

THE GREATER THE RISK

OF UNDERARM ODOUR

USE

LIQUID

ODO-RO-NO

FOR COMPLETE UNDERARM PROTECTION

Odo-ro-no Liquid in two strengths. REGULAR (lasts for seven days). INSTANT (three days). Medium and small sizes.

In hot weather especially
Service girls
should remember . . .

THE GREATER THE STRAIN

THE GREATER THE RISK

OF UNDERARM STAIN

USE

LIQUID

ODO-RO-NO

FOR COMPLETE UNDERARM PROTECTION

Odo-ro-no Liquid in two strengths. REGULAR (lasts for seven days). INSTANT (three days). Medium and small sizes.

Left: A pair of wartime adverts for Odo-ro-no, 'The greater the strain the greater the risk of underarm stain', *Picture Post*, 1942.

Opposite page: Tampax advert, 'It makes life simpler', *Housewife*, May 1944.

The true creator is never idle. Though manufacture of perfumes and many of our beauty preparations is no longer possible, dreams of fresh loveliness and perfection already exist in the minds of our experts. Novel and exciting perfumes and preparations that will add fresh laurels to the fame of Coty when peace permits the realization of our post-war plans.

Both American and British governments initially saw beauty products as inessential luxuries, but both were to change their tune. Make-up came to be appreciated as essential for morale as were cigarettes and beer. In fact make-up came to be positively advocated with such copy as 'we must never lower our standards to the enemy' and 'never forget good looks and good morale go hand-in-hand'. Tattoo echoing the now iconic pronouncement with its own 'England expects these days that every woman shall be a beauty'. The Americans took things one step further with their wartime poster heroine, Rosie the Riveter, with her henna red hair, the reddest of lips and equally red nails.

Yardley urged women to 'put your best face forward' and Eve Shampoo assured them that 'appearance still counts'. Tangee Lipstick advertisements, targeted at the Services were headed 'Beauty on duty':

On duty she must look smart but not painted.
That's why Tangee is the invariable choice of all women on National Service.

125

Prepare for HIS Leave!

OF COURSE you must look your charming best — and the surest way to do justice to your beauty is to crown it with a Eugene Wave. He'll tell you that he's never seen you looking so attractive — and he'll mean it! Make an appointment today.

THERE IS A EUGENE / SACHET SUITABLE
FOR EVERY TYPE & TEXTURE OF HAIR

● See the name and trademark on every Sachet
● See a Eugene Sachet wrapped round every curler

Put your best face forward...

Because the loveliness they give seems truly natural, Yardley beauty-things are more precious today than ever.

Remember, they still have all the qualities you know and trust.

Yardley

* If you have any war-time beauty problems write to Mary Potter, the Yardley Beauty Consultant. She will be very glad to help.

3 3   O L D   B O N D   S T R E E T   L O N D O N

Above: Eugene, 'Prepare for HIS Leave!', *Picture Post*, December 1939.

Above right: Yardley, 'Put your best face forward', *Housewife*, June 1944.

And along with them keeping up their own morale it was suggested that there was a need for women to look good to keep up the morale of their menfolk, particularly those at the front. Women might never reach the heights of attractiveness of wartime pin-ups hanging in forces' mess, or even adorning their planes, but they should work on it. Eugene Wave advertisements urged its use 'to make him feel good when he was home on leave' and 'prepare for HIS leave!', for which 'you must look your charming best.' Make-up certainly lifted the morale of many G.I.s based in, or passing through, Britain on their way to war zones, with resulting gifts of silk stockings, chewing gum, and the occasional offspring!

Odo-ro-no found its own niche in helping the war effort as women were to find themselves in novel surroundings, oftimes crowded in with strangers, and certainly working under stress – all bringing with them increased sweating. The company associated itself with keeping heavy uniforms fresh and similar patriotic actions. Sanitary towels were also quick to exploit wartime conditions as with Tampax 'helping to make life simpler when you're involved in action'; and Rendell's making it a woman's duty to serve her country by using its products.

In fact the beauty industry kept surprisingly afloat during the war and was actually to benefit, either directly or indirectly, from wartime activities., as with the later civilian use of aerosols developed as an insecticide for the troops. Women may well have had to make-do without powder puffs, with lipsticks in cardboard and paper rather than in show-off metal cases, with drab containers for creams and oftimes with crude homemade substitutes, but make-up they did. To what extent it kept up theirs and their men's morale is questionable, but it certainly helped the manufacturers to weather the war, to keep their brand names vibrant, and possibly to lift hearts by promises of the goodies that were to come once peace was made.

Epilogue

The latter part of the nineteenth century into the early years of the twentieth saw a fever of activity, of experiment and innovation of beauty products – chemistry students in their lodgings, ambitious young women in their kitchens, artisans in their tool shops, perfumIers in their backrooms, laboratory workers in soap factories, local chemists in their shops, make-up artists in theatres and in movie studios – all contributed to the cosmic expansion of the beauty products market. Many of the people involved had a genuine desire to contribute to people's health and through this to their attractiveness, to produce products that were less harmful, products that were easier to use; but others were chancers, seeing a gap in the market or climbing on to a particular fashionable band wagon.

Most enterprises started out with, at the most, a couple of products, expanding their range, until eventually everyone was trying to sell everything – nail varnish specialists selling face cream, skin specialists selling mascara, cosmeticians going into health care, and so on, although few companies found as much success over the

POMEROY
SKIN FOOD
HELPS THE PLAIN
IMPROVES THE FAIR

Poster for Pomeroy 'Skin Food',
Edward McKnight Kauffer,
c. 1926.

whole of the range as they had with their original product that had made them a household name, as exemplified by Yardley's with its traditional flower seller advertising its perfume, extending its range into cosmetics for women, and later for men, its advertising enlivened by Reco Capey.

As with so many products, in the twentieth century, success or likely potential for growth, brought about much buying and selling of enterprises – Unilever gobbling up Cheseborough, Ponds, Rimmel, and Elizabeth Arden amongst others; Procter and Gamble taking over Max Factor, Clairol, Wella and Gillette; L'Oréal snapping up Maybelline, and Lancôme eventually owning well over thirty brands.

The advertising of beauty products started mainly without image, or what image there was taking up a modest part of the advertising space. Companies, early on, seemed to find it necessary to carry dense copy, explaining the make up of the product, blinding the reader with science, sometimes mere mumbo jumbo, with recommendations from the medical profession as to the miracle results that might be achieved by using the product. If the advertisement was pictorial it tended to be an image of the packed goods (in cardboard, pot, glass or metal), sometimes with the company trademark or logo.

Over time copy retreated and the imagery grew, the references or sometimes faces of the medical profession giving way to pictures of celebrities, stars of first stage, then radio and cinema and to sportsmen, in Britain mainly footballers and cricketers.

Right: 'Christmas gifts by Avon!',
advert for Avon Cosmetics, *Woman's
Own*, November 1969.

As branding grew, the brand name came often to replace in size the name of the manufacturer, which largely appeared in reduced font, hidden away at the bottom of the advertisement. Eventually, for brand names that came to dominate their particular market, it became sufficient merely to have a glamour photograph or striking sketch with the brand name superimposed, copy reduced to a tagline of few words. Market success brought arrogance.

1920's advertising of beauty products focused on the 'flapper'; the 1930s on the healthy, sportive, independent woman; the 1940s on the feisty courageous contributor to the war effort; the 1960s introduced sex; whilst the late 1960s moved on to the youth market, when making-up became having fun. Advertising to the masses (as well as to the elite), was facilitated by the explosion of magazines for women and girls, giving them role models to emulate; aided by the increasing use of photography. For a good deal of this advertising the key slant was French (even cream spelt crème); and Paris needed to be seen somewhere in the space (along with London and New York).

Few artists made their names, or were even named, in beauty product advertising, perhaps Tom Eckersley with his work for Gillette and Reco Capey for Yardley; it was but another string to the bows of Francis Marshall and René Bouché, both better known for their work with fashion; only René Gruau, perhaps, standing out, for his iconic 'rouge baiser' images. It was Gruau who might have supplied the answer to Geoffrey Jones' question:

Why do people pay so much for inessentials where ingredients are so small a proportion of price?

When Gruau was asked about his attitude to working in advertising he replied:

I want advertising to be refined and graphic and for it visually to surpass reality... I think images should make you dream.

And that is what the beauty industry counted on!

Bibliography

1999   Caroline Cox, *Good Hair Days*, Quartet Books Virago.

2003   Lindy Woodhead, *War Paint*, Virago.

2009   Madeleine Marsh, *Compacts and Cosmetics*,
        Pen & Sword History.

2010   Geoffrey Jones, *Beauty Imagined*, OUP.

2012   Sarah Jane Downing, *Beauty and Cosmetics, 1550–1950*,
        Shire Books.

2015   Lisa Eldridge, *Face Paint*, Abrams Image N.Y.

Ref. journals: *Commercial Art* and *Art & Industry*.

The bulk of the illustrations come from a private collection.